DEADLY DISEASES AND EPIDEMICS

LYME DISEASE

Anthrax

Cholera

HIV/AIDS

Influenza

Lyme Disease

Malaria

Mononucleosis

Polio

Syphilis

Toxic Shock Syndrome

Tuberculosis

Typhoid Fever

DEADLY DISEASES AND EPIDEMICS

LYME DISEASE

Len Yannielli

CONSULTING EDITOR
I. Edward Alcamo
Distinguished Teaching Professor of Microbiology,
SUNY Farmingdale

FOREWORD BY
David Heymann
World Health Organization

CHELSEA HOUSE
P U B L I S H E R S
A Haights Cross Communications Company

P h i l a d e l p h i a

Dedication

We dedicate the books in the DEADLY DISEASES AND EPIDEMICS series to Ed Alcamo, whose wit, charm, intelligence, and commitment to biology education were second to none.

CHELSEA HOUSE PUBLISHERS

VP, NEW PRODUCT DEVELOPMENT Sally Cheney
DIRECTOR OF PRODUCTION Kim Shinners
CREATIVE MANAGER Takeshi Takahashi
MANUFACTURING MANAGER Diann Grasse

Staff for Lyme Disease

ASSOCIATE EDITOR Beth Reger
PRODUCTION EDITOR Megan Emery
PHOTO EDITOR Sarah Bloom
SERIES DESIGNER Terry Mallon
COVER DESIGNER Keith Trego
LAYOUT 21st Century Publishing and Communications, Inc.

A Haights Cross Communications Company
http://www.chelseahouse.com

First Printing

1 3 5 7 9 8 6 4 2

Library of Congress Cataloging-in-Publication Data applied for.

ISBN 0-7910-7463-3

Table of Contents

Foreword

In the 1960s, infectious diseases—which had terrorized generations— were tamed. Building on a century of discoveries, the leading killers of Americans both young and old were being prevented with new vaccines or cured with new medicines. The risk of death from pneumonia, tuberculosis, meningitis, influenza, whooping cough, and diphtheria declined dramatically. New vaccines lifted the fear that summer would bring polio, and a global campaign was approaching the global eradication of smallpox. New pesticides like DDT cleared mosquitoes from homes and fields, thus reducing the incidence of malaria which was present in the southern United States and a leading killer of children worldwide. New technologies produced safe drinking water and removed the risk of cholera and other water-borne diseases. Science seemed unstoppable. Disease seemed destined to almost disappear.

But the euphoria of the 1960s has evaporated.

Microbes fight back. Those causing diseases like TB and malaria evolved resistance to cheap and effective drugs. The mosquito evolved the ability to defuse pesticides. New diseases emerged, including AIDS, Legionnaires, and Lyme disease. And diseases which have not been seen in decades re-emerge, as the hantavirus did in the Navajo Nation in 1993. Technology itself actually created new health risks. The global transportation network, for example, meant that diseases like West Nile virus could spread beyond isolated regions in distant countries and quickly become global threats. Even modern public health protections sometimes failed, as they did in Milwaukee, Wisconsin in 1993 which resulted in 400,000 cases of the digestive system illness cryptosporidiosis. And, more recently, the threat from smallpox, a disease completely eradicated, has returned along with other potential bioterrorism weapons such as anthrax.

The lesson is that the fight against infectious diseases will never end.

In this constant struggle against disease, we as individuals have a weapon that does not require vaccines or drugs, the warehouse of knowledge. We learn from the history of science that "modern" beliefs can be wrong. In this series of books, for example, you will learn that diseases like syphilis were once thought to be caused by eating potatoes. The invention of the microscope set science on the right path. There are more positive lessons from history. For example, smallpox was eliminated by vaccinating everyone who had come in contact with an infected person. This "ring" approach to controlling smallpox is still the preferred method for confronting a smallpox outbreak should the disease be intentionally reintroduced.

At the same time, we are constantly adding new drugs, new vaccines, and new information to the warehouse. Recently, the entire human genome was decoded. So too was the genome of the parasite that causes malaria. Perhaps by looking at the microbe and the victim through the lens of genetics we will to be able to discover new ways of fighting malaria, still the leading killer of children in many countries.

Because of the knowledge gained about such diseases as AIDS, entire new classes of anti-retroviral drugs have been developed. But resistance to all these drugs has already been detected, so we know that AIDS drug development must continue.

Education, experimentation, and the discoveries which grow out of them are the best tools to protect health. Opening this book may put you on the path of discovery. I hope so, because new vaccines, new antibiotics, new technologies and, most importantly, new scientists are needed now more than ever if we are to remain on the winning side of this struggle with microbes.

David Heymann
Executive Director
Communicable Diseases Section
World Health Organization
Geneva, Switzerland

1

Two Case Histories: An Introduction to Lyme Disease

The future of infectious disease will be very dull.
—**Sir Frank Macfarlane Burnet, 1960 Winner of the Nobel Prize in Physiology or Medicine**

Each year, about 15,000 cases of Lyme disease are reported in the United States, making it our number one vector-borne, or animal carried, disease (Figures 1.1 and 1.2). Surprisingly, Lyme disease was not listed as an official disease category by the Centers for Disease Control and Prevention (CDC) until 1982.

The public is still unaware of many of the aspects of Lyme disease— e.g., its symptoms, its cause, its method of transmission (is it contagious?). However, there are many aspects of Lyme disease that are known. For example, we know that a certain type of tick spreads the disease (see Chapter 4), and that Lyme disease is actually caused by bacteria (Chapter 3). There is a vaccine, but it is not presently available (see Chapter 8). More research needs to be done on the interaction of the animals involved in the **pathogenesis** of the disease, assessing the role of the environment, and determining the effectiveness of different preventive measures (see Chapters 5 and 9).

The case histories that follow are a good place to begin our study of Lyme disease. These stories will introduce the many symptoms

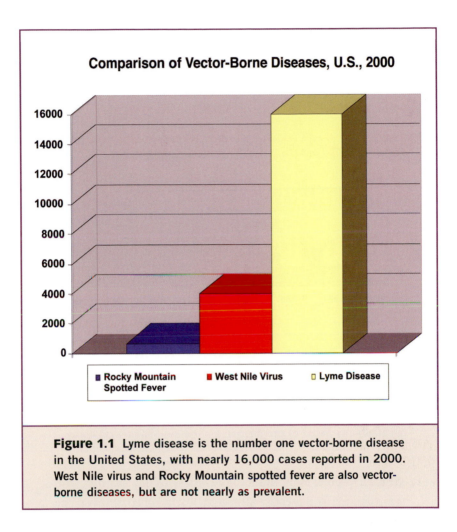

Comparison of Vector-Borne Diseases, U.S., 2000

- ■ Rocky Mountain Spotted Fever
- ■ West Nile Virus
- □ Lyme Disease

Figure 1.1 Lyme disease is the number one vector-borne disease in the United States, with nearly 16,000 cases reported in 2000. West Nile virus and Rocky Mountain spotted fever are also vector-borne diseases, but are not nearly as prevalent.

involved and the difficulties faced by biomedical professionals in diagnosing the disease. Both of these stories are based upon real experiences with the disease.

CASE I: MARIA

Maria Santiago had been feeling under the weather lately. She had recently recovered from the worst case of the flu she ever had. Although her stiff neck and fever had subsided, she still felt tired. The only thing she wanted to do was stay home, but

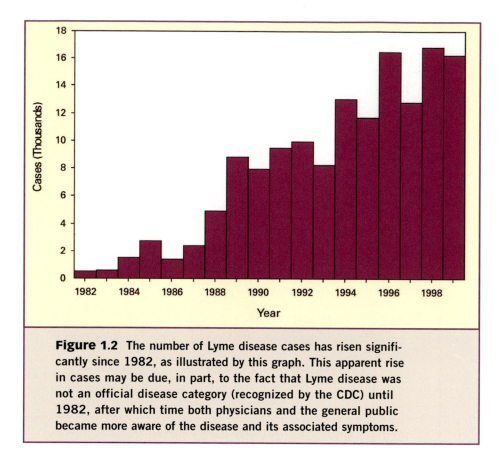

Figure 1.2 The number of Lyme disease cases has risen significantly since 1982, as illustrated by this graph. This apparent rise in cases may be due, in part, to the fact that Lyme disease was not an official disease category (recognized by the CDC) until 1982, after which time both physicians and the general public became more aware of the disease and its associated symptoms.

she had to go to human biology class with her mother, who was also taking the class. Although Maria ached all over, she did not want to disappoint her mother.

Maria tried to remember the last time she felt healthy. It was at the picnic at the local park. She remembered running after a Frisbee and diving into the shrubs after an errant throw. Funny, she thought, that none of her friends had caught the flu.

As Maria got in the car to go to class, her mother noticed a red rash on the side and back of Maria's left thigh. Maria told her mother that she had seen it in her bathroom mirror two days earlier and that the rash did not itch. They drove to class, not thinking about it again.

Maria and her mother entered the classroom and sat down. The instructor was writing the topics for the day's lecture on the blackboard: "Lyme Disease: Epidemiology, The Bacteria, The Tick, The Habitat, The History, Treatment, and Prevention."

The instructor asked if anyone in the class had Lyme disease. Maria was surprised to see a student raise his hand. Neither she, nor her mother, had ever heard of Lyme disease before. What really surprised her was when the instructor asked if any of the students knew someone with Lyme disease. Five people raised their hands.

The instructor began showing slides related to Lyme disease. Then, he listed the symptoms of Lyme disease: flu-like symptoms, a reddening of the eyes, a stiff neck, and a large circular red rash. The rash was similar to the one Maria had.

Maria and her mother talked to the instructor after class. The instructor recommended that Maria see a doctor and have a blood antibody test done. Within days, Maria learned she had Lyme disease.

CASE II: FRED

Fred and his doctor determined he had Lyme disease fairly quickly. Other people in Fred's neighborhood had the disease, and Fred was aware of the symptoms. He was not an outdoor person, so he did not know how he became infected. However, Fred and his wife often let their cat sleep in their bed, and the doctor said a tick carrying the Lyme disease bacteria probably migrated from the cat and attached to him.

After a year of antibiotic treatment, Fred finally felt healthy again. However, about two years later, his neck began to feel chronically sore. The usual sore neck remedies did not relieve the pain. He began having headaches, muscle and joint pain, and facial twitching. He also started feeling depressed. Fred's doctor diagnosed him with chronic Lyme disease.

Because of his chronic disease, Fred had to adjust to a modified lifestyle. He had to have medication constantly delivered

THE FUTURE OF INFECTIOUS DISEASE

During the period between the 1850s and the beginning of World War I (1914), also known as the "Golden Age of Microbiology," scientists such as Louis Pasteur and Robert Koch successfully showed that specific diseases could be linked to specific microbes. By the early 1900s, the most deadly diseases—e.g., bubonic plague, diphtheria, flu, smallpox, and tuberculosis—were linked to specific pathogens. The development of vaccines against these pathogens helped many people prevent illness and, in some cases, death.

In 1798, Edward Jenner tested the first vaccine against smallpox. During the Golden Age, other vaccines were developed. Then, in the 1940s, antibiotics helped those already afflicted with certain diseases. The present and future of disease control looked very promising. The prospect of totally eliminating such diseases as smallpox was becoming a reality. Euphoria arose in some scientific circles, so much so that by the late 1960s, some medical schools actually contemplated eliminating medical microbiology from their curricula.

There was a sense that the battle against infectious disease had been won. However, new diseases emerged during the latter half of the twentieth century, changing that optimistic forecast. The rampant spread of such diseases as AIDS, Ebola virus, hepatitis C, and Legionnaires' disease complicated matters for scientists. Antibiotic resistance and the threat of bioterrorism also added to the problem. In short, microorganisms, and the animals with which they interact, are always evolving—that is, changing with the passage of time. These challenges require constant scientific research, discovery, and development. Lyme disease shows us that research in the area of infectious disease must continue and will remain an exciting endeavor.

intravenously. He also became easily angered and depressed. His doctor explained that toxins from the Lyme bacteria can affect the nervous system and cause depression.

Fred's doctor suggested that he join the local Lyme disease support group, which he did. The discussions with other Lyme disease patients helped him better understand his medical situation and the adjustments he could make. Taking a walk every morning for exercise helped him through the day. He better understood Lyme disease, and his life began to improve.

Although the names have been changed, both of these stories are based upon actual cases. As they show, Lyme disease can manifest itself in various ways, and have different effects on the physical and emotional health of its victims. For these reasons, Lyme disease is a difficult disease for health care professionals to diagnose.

2

The History of Lyme Disease

Chance favors the prepared mind.

—Louis Pasteur

Determining the exact origin of a disease is difficult, particularly for diseases that have been with us for millennia—e.g., plague or syphilis. Debates rage in both scientific and popular publications as to the exact origins of such diseases. Not surprisingly, discovering the true origins of Lyme disease has also proved difficult.

EARLY HISTORY

In 1883, Alfred Buchwald, a German physician from Breslau, Germany, wrote about a skin disorder that had similarities to Lyme disease. That disease is now called "acrodermatitis chronica atrophicans." Another physician, Arvid Afzelius, reported to the Swedish Society of Dermatology about an expanding rash he had observed. He did not publish his findings until 1920, but theorized that the rash had originated from an *Ixodes* sheep tick.

In the 1920s and 1930s, there were again reports about an expanding red rash, called erythema migrans (EM), and descriptions of some of the other symptoms that would later be associated with Lyme disease. At the time, however, the symptoms were not striking enough to denote a new disease. Also, the number of identified cases was very low.

Around 1940, cases of swollen joints, particularly of the knee, were reported on Long Island, New York. Many of these patients were from the Montauk Point area of Long Island, and thus this local phenomenon was referred to as Montauk knee. In 1969, a Wisconsin physician recognized erythema migrans in a patient, and successfully treated the patient with penicillin. Again, none of these cases suggested the emergence of a new disease, at least not yet.

A CASE OF MISTAKEN IDENTITY?

Determining the etiology, or cause, of a disease is almost always a difficult task. With Lyme disease, the story begins along the southeast coastline of Connecticut. In 1975, Judith Mench of Old Lyme, Connecticut, sent her eight-year-old daughter, Amy, out for Halloween. When Amy returned with a swollen knee, her parents took her to a doctor. The doctor thought she may have osteomyelitis, a bacterial infection of the bone. Amy was

WHAT'S IN A NAME?

When cases of arthritis first appeared in Lyme, Connecticut, the disease was called Lyme arthritis, a name that included both the location and the symptoms of the malady. Soon thereafter, Allen Steere, a Yale University research scientist, challenged the arthritis diagnosis. The successful search for the infectious agent would have an impact on the naming of the disease.

Willy Burgdorfer's discovery of the spirochete infectious agent in the *Borrelia* genus made a large impression on the scientific community. The name Lyme borreliosis soon began being used to refer to the new disease in both scientific journals and the news media. But the evolution of the disease's name did not end there.

Often, diseases are named after the person who discovered them. For example, *Rickettsia* was named after its discoverer Howard Taylor Ricketts. Because of this naming pattern in the past, people began referring to the disease caused by *Borrelia burgdorferi* as Lyme disease. They thought the discoverer's name was Lyme. However, naming the disease after the town where the first cases were revealed is also a time-honored tradition in science. By the early 1990s, both the scientific community and the media agreed on the name, and it has become permanent.

taken to Lawrence & Memorial Hospital in New London, Connecticut, for intravenous doses of antibiotics.

The tests for bacterial and viral infections were negative, so Amy was taken off antibiotics and sent home with aspirin, the typical treatment for juvenile rheumatoid arthritis (JRA). Judith immediately questioned this diagnosis, because neither JRA nor any kind of arthritis was common in her family history. Furthermore, she knew three other children in the neighborhood had also been diagnosed with JRA. She knew arthritis was not contagious. After the passage of much time, Judith's thinking was proven correct. Amy did not have JRA; she had Lyme disease.

Polly Murray of Lyme, Connecticut, had a very different experience. She remembered having rashes and other symptoms typical of Lyme disease as early as 1959. Her symptoms suggested rheumatic fever, an inflammatory disease. At other times, she had headaches and stiff joints. Doctors told her she might have lupus, a disease that affects the skin and joints. She insisted that she must have something else, but doctors dismissed her as a hypochondriac. She kept a journal of her health problems through the years and began to research her condition.

Over time, Murray's entire family also began exhibiting the same symptoms. Doctors implied that the family was mimicking what they described as her "neurotic behavior" patterns. The doctors were wrong. Polly Murray had Lyme disease.

AN OUTBREAK OF ARTHRITIS

In fall 1975, the Connecticut Department of Health Services received a number of calls about people—mostly children from Lyme and Old Lyme, Connecticut—who had arthritic symptoms and a red rash. Most of the calls were from three adjacent towns (Lyme, Old Lyme, and East Haddam) along the southeastern border of the Connecticut River. **Epidemiologists**, scientists who study disease patterns (**epidemiology** is the study of disease prevalence), called this grouping of cases a cluster. The epidemiologists had a specific geographic area on which to

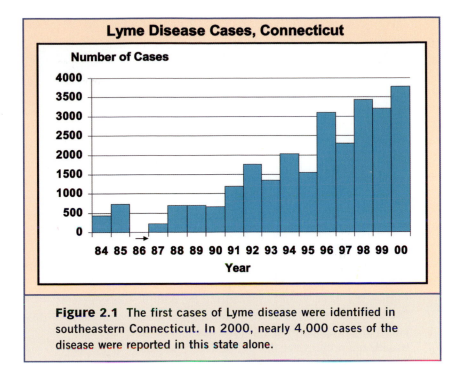

Figure 2.1 The first cases of Lyme disease were identified in southeastern Connecticut. In 2000, nearly 4,000 cases of the disease were reported in this state alone.

focus so they could learn more about these cases (Figure 2.1). They needed to determine similarities in the cases—e.g., whether they were reported during a specific time of year, the age and gender of the people affected, and any hereditary factors. They also needed to look at the area where the calls came from, including the **flora**, the **fauna**, and the **topography** of the land.

Investigating the Cluster

Allen Steere, a researcher at Yale University who was interested in rheumatology (the study of muscles, joints, and connective tissues) learned about the cluster of cases. Although he noted that the symptoms resembled those of arthritis, he questioned the diagnosis of JRA. It would be the beginning of a medical odyssey for Steere that would exemplify Louis Pasteur's adage, "Chance favors the prepared mind."

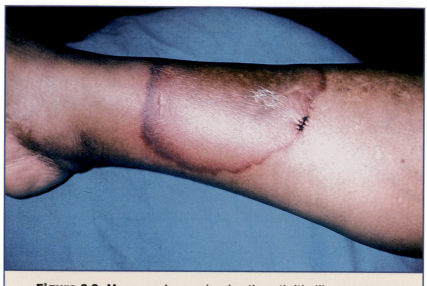

Figure 2.2 Many people experiencing the arthritic-like symptoms that were later found to be the result of Lyme disease also experienced a red, circular rash, like the one shown here. The rash usually has a bull's-eye-like appearance and occurs at the site where the tick attaches to the skin.

Steere began a phone survey of the young people who had complained of the arthritic-like symptoms. He soon found that a significant number of people reporting these symptoms had also experienced a red circular rash (Figure 2.2). Steere became more and more convinced that the rash did not fit the usual JRA scenario. He thought the cause may be an **infectious** agent, but he did not know where to find it.

Determining the Source of Infection

Because Old Lyme, Lyme, and East Haddam were situated along the Connecticut River, an area with considerable wetlands, (Figure 2.3), Steere first thought that the drinking water might harbor an infectious agent. However, he inferred that the cause was not in the water and was not contagious because not every member of the victims' families was affected. Steere also

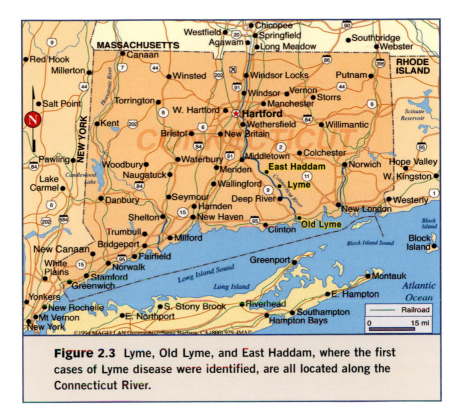

Figure 2.3 Lyme, Old Lyme, and East Haddam, where the first cases of Lyme disease were identified, are all located along the Connecticut River.

noticed that most of the cases occurred in late spring and summer. Researchers at the Connecticut Agricultural Station, Steere, and other scientists at Yale began considering the possibility of an **arthropod** being the **vector**, or carrier, of the disease. Insects, being the largest category in this group, were considered.

Steere had heard from a colleague of an erythema migrans-like rash in arthritis patients in northern Europe. He also read in an early 1900s European textbook about a large, red, expanding rash on a sheep herder that was caused not by an insect but by a tick. Furthermore, he found that some victims in Connecticut recalled a tick attachment before the onset of symptoms.

Steere and other researchers then focused on finding which species of tick was involved. Connecticut is home to 22 different species of ticks. Wood ticks and dog ticks are the most common. The researchers noticed that the cluster of cases occurred on one side of the river. That side was inhabited by a particular black-legged tick called *Ixodes scapularis,* which is popularly referred to as a deer tick (Figure 2.4).

MUSEUM TICKS

Museums have played an important role in the study of the past, especially when investigating problems of natural history. Quite often, problems that have vexed scientists for years have been solved by the discovery of a long forgotten fossil in a museum's "junk drawer" of natural artifacts.

In 1990, Dave Pershing and Paul Rys of Yale University's School of Medicine wanted to know whether museums could play the same role in discovering the origin of Lyme disease. They were busy honing the powerful molecular tool of **polymerase chain reaction** (PCR) technology. Perhaps this relatively new (in 1990) DNA technology could be combined with science's time-honored use of museums to shed more light on Lyme disease's history.

They obtained 102 alcohol-preserved deer ticks, collected between 1945 and 1951, from the Museum of Comparative Zoology in Cambridge, Massachusetts. Most of the ticks were collected from islands off the coast of Massachusetts and Connecticut. Other deer ticks from Florida and South Carolina, as well as dog ticks, were used for comparative purposes.

Pershing and Rys tested the ticks for a specific DNA sequence known to be characteristic only of *Borrelia burgdorferi,* the cause of Lyme disease. Although most turned up negative, the DNA sequence specific for the bacteria showed up in 13 specimens from Montauk Point and Hither Hills, Long Island.

Although the number of specimens tested was small, they were able to learn more about the history of Lyme disease by combining relatively new molecular techniques with a classic time-honored use of museum specimens.

Figure 2.4 The black-legged, or deer tick (*Ixodes scapularis)* at the top and the dog tick (*Dermacaentor variabilis*), bottom. Only the black-legged tick is a vector for Lyme disease. When a tick feeds on the blood of another organism, the Lyme bacteria can be transferred.

Finding the Cause

These discoveries in 1975–1976 are mostly associated with the discovery of Lyme disease. However, no known etiological or infectious agents were identified at this time. Some European doctors had successfully used certain antibiotics to treat patients who had the red rash. The researchers focused on finding the bacterium that was causing the rash.

In the early 1980s, Willy Burgdorfer, a world-renowned tick expert, was researching Rocky Mountain spotted fever, which at that time was the number one **tick-borne** illness in the United States. While working in Montana in 1981, he received some ticks from an area in New York that was known for Rocky Mountain spotted fever. While examining these ticks under a microscope, he saw long, slender, twisted bacteria in the category called spirochetes (spi'ro-ketes). Figure 2.5 shows an example of a spirochete.

Burgdorfer knew that spirochetes had never before been associated with *Ixodes scapularis* ticks. He also knew that the bacteria *Rickettsia*, not a spirochete, caused Rocky Mountain spotted fever. He was aware that Lyme arthritis occurred in the area where the ticks were collected and that antibiotics were generally effective against spirochetes.

Soon after Burgdorfer's discovery, Steere isolated the same long, slender bacteria from patients with Lyme arthritis. The spirochete, an etiological agent for Lyme arthritis, was named *Borrelia burgdorferi* in honor of Burgdorfer.

While some basic questions had now been answered about Lyme disease, scientists still did not know its origins. A journey into the earliest years of the nation would reveal that answer.

EXAMINING THE PAST TO DETERMINE THE FUTURE

Origins in the United States—A Theory

One theory on the origin of Lyme disease places ecosystem imbalance as its centerpiece, combined with the emergence of the United States as a nation-state. Early European descriptions of

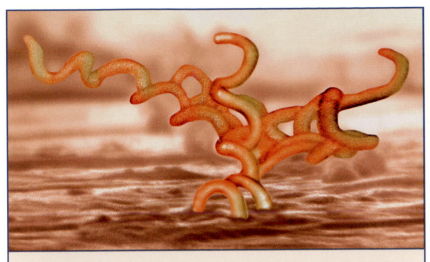

Figure 2.5 *Borrelia burgdorferi*, the bacterium that causes Lyme disease, is classified as a spirochete bacterium because of its spiral shape. The bacteria shown here, which causes syphilis, is an example of a spirochete.

the erythema migrans (EM) rash are well documented, albeit without the long-term heart and nervous system effects associated with chronic Lyme disease. Because no such early documentation exists for North America, nobody could yet explain how Lyme disease came to the United States or how it became so debilitating.

During the American Revolutionary War (1776–1783) the French, English, and American colonists intermingled. King George sent German Hessian mercenaries (soldiers for hire) to fight. The British had a problem with obtaining the necessary food and supplies to maintain the German troops far from England. The British decided to temporarily set up camp for these troops on islands off the coasts of Connecticut and Massachusetts, because these islands were still plentiful with a ready source of food—the white-tailed deer.

Given the early history of the EM rash and *Ixodes* tick in northern Europe, it is theorized that some Hessian troops transported the tick, and bacteria with them, from Europe to the United States. The ticks then adapted to local fauna, such as deer and small mammals, providing the necessary ingredients for the life cycle of the disease. The disease was most likely transported from the islands to the mainland by birds. When the secondary forests began to appear in the 1900s, along with much larger deer populations, all the factors were in place for the *Ixodes scapularis* tick's life cycle to take hold on the mainland.

Landscape Changes

Early colonial journals noted the presence of ticks. The forests and their attendant wildlife were plentiful. Then the clearing of the land for herd animals and agricultural purposes began in earnest. In Connecticut, for example, 80% of the forests were leveled between 1700 and 1900. The only forests left were in wetlands or high on mountain ridges. The latter were maintained as a source of wood for charcoal, which was used extensively during this period for heating and cooking.

The changing landscape had far-reaching consequences for wildlife. Forest animals lost their habitats. Deer, vital to the life cycle of the deer tick *Ixodes scapularis*, lost their forest retreats, which are especially important for the survival of their young. Farmers hunted the deer for food and also to protect their crops from being eaten. By 1900, very few deer were left in Connecticut.

The decline in the deer population affected predators, such as timber wolves and mountain lions, in two ways: they rapidly lost their prey, and they became increasingly hunted by farmers who saw them as competitors for deer meat. The last wolf was extirpated from Connecticut in the late nineteenth century.

Ecosystem Imbalance

In the beginning of the twentieth century, farming gradually moved to the Midwest. Connecticut started being naturally refor- ested. For example, it is quite typical to come upon rock walls, which used to mark the edge of farmers' fields, right in the middle of secondary forests. These woodlands, however, were, and are, inundated by both urban and suburban sprawl—helter-skelter growth that fragments forest areas with roads and houses.

These seemingly unrelated events—extinction of predators and reforestation with fragmentation due to sprawl—have contributed heavily to a large white-tailed deer population (20 million nationwide and 76,000 in Connecticut alone). Deer favor woodland edges. Because white-tailed deer are crucial to the life cycle of *Ixodes scapularis*, these events have brought about an **ecological imbalance** that can be directly attributed to the emergence of Lyme disease.

However, the exact origin of Lyme disease is, to date, unknown. As more information is discovered about Lyme disease, theories about its origins will continue to evolve.

LYME DISEASE TIMELINE

1975— Connecticut Department of Health Services alerted about cases of a new disease involving arthritis-like symptoms and erythema migrans rash.

1976— Phases or stages of Lyme arthritis recognized.

1981— *Ixodes scapularis* tick found with spirochetes named *Borrelia burgdorferi*.

Disease referred to as Lyme borreliosis.

1982— Centers for Disease Control and Prevention recognizes and defines Lyme disease.

1988— Lyme Disease Foundation established.

1989— Outer surface protein (OspA) discovered and cloned.

1990s— Lyme disease name commonly used in both popular and scientific presses.

1990–1992— Vaccinations protect mice against Lyme disease.

1998— Food and Drug Administration approves Lyme disease vaccine.

2002— Lyme disease vaccine production halted.

3

The Bacteria

I see little beasties.

—Anton van Leeuwenhoek (1632–1723)

ETIOLOGY AND TAXONOMY

Ask the average person what causes Lyme disease and the person will usually say "deer tick" or "Lyme tick." Many people believe that ticks cause Lyme disease, because much of the publicity around Lyme disease has focused on the deer tick. Most preventive measures focus on avoiding tick attachment.

The infectious or etiological agent of Lyme disease in the United States is not the tick but a species of bacteria called *Borrelia burgdorferi* (Figure 3.1) that lives inside the tick. There are also over one hundred different *Borrelia burgdorferi* **strains** (a further taxonomic division beyond the species). There are two other Lyme disease pathogenic or disease-causing species in the world—*Borrelia afzelii* and *Borrelia garinii*. Because these two species, which include over three hundred strains, are found in Europe and Asia, this chapter will focus on *Borrelia burgdorferi*, which is the species found most often in the United States. Lyme disease in the United States is known for its arthritic symptoms, whereas in Europe it is known more for its neurological symptoms. There are other diseases caused by different species of *Borrelia* as well.

MORPHOLOGY AND STRUCTURES

Although there are many variations, bacteria come in three basic morphologies, or shapes: rods, spheres, and spirals. *Borrelia burgdorferi*,

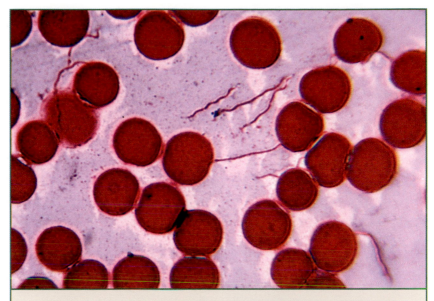

Figure 3.1 *Borrelia burgdorferi* is the organism that causes Lyme disease. They can be seen in this electron micrograph between the red blood cells. Recall that *Borrelia burgdorferi* are spirochetes, so they have a spiral shape.

which causes Lyme disease, is a spiral or corkscrew-shaped bacteria, known as a spirochete (recall Figure 2.5 on Page 23).

Borrelia burgdorferi is one of the longest spirochetes, ranging from 20 to 30 micrometers in length. It is also the narrowest spirochete at 0.2 to 0.3 micrometers wide. Although it is large by bacterial standards, it would take 1,500 *Borrelia burgdorferi* placed end to end to equal one inch. Its cell envelope consists of both an outer and an inner membrane. These membranes are composed of a combination of lipids and proteins called lipoproteins.

Some bacteria have flagella, whip-like structures that stretch outward from the cells. The flagella help the bacterium move in its environment. *Borrelia burgdorferi* have flagella, but they are located between the outer and inner membranes. These structures, called endoflagella, help propel the bacteria in a

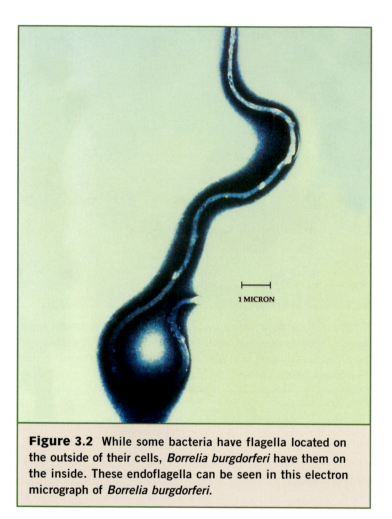

Figure 3.2 While some bacteria have flagella located on the outside of their cells, *Borrelia burgdorferi* have them on the inside. These endoflagella can be seen in this electron micrograph of *Borrelia burgdorferi*.

corkscrew fashion (Figure 3.2). Flagella allow the bacteria to move through the tissues of their **hosts**.

GENETIC MAKEUP

The **genome** of *Borrelia burgdorferi* consists of 1.5 million nitrogen bases in its DNA molecules. *Borrelia burgdorferi* has one chromosome of 950,000 nitrogen bases and 21 **plasmids** consisting of 550,000 nitrogen bases. Although this number is considered small by bacterial standards, it is not unusual

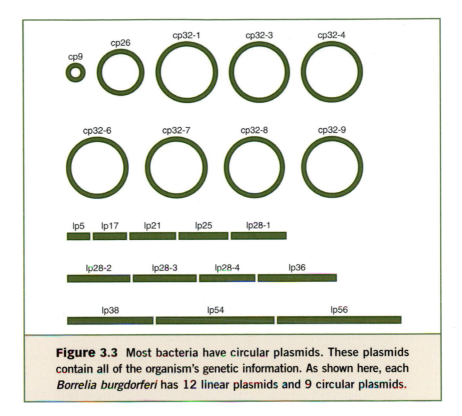

Figure 3.3 Most bacteria have circular plasmids. These plasmids contain all of the organism's genetic information. As shown here, each *Borrelia burgdorferi* has 12 linear plasmids and 9 circular plasmids.

for a spirochete. For example, *Treponema pallidum*, the spirochete infectious agent that causes syphilis, has 1.14 million nitrogen bases.

There are several unique features of the *Borrelia burgdorferi* genome. Its largest chromosome, 950 kilobases and 853 genes, is linear. The vast majority of bacteria have a circular genome. Also, 12 of its 21 plasmids are linear. In most bacteria, plasmids are all circular (Figure 3.3).

The bacterium's genome codes for many of the lipoproteins on its outer surface are called outer surface proteins A through F (OspA-F). Apparently, these surface proteins allow the *Borrelia burgdorferi* spirochete to survive in animals as varied as ticks and mammals. Some of their surface proteins go through extensive molecular changes called antigen shifting.

This continuous change in antigenic outer surface proteins poses a particular challenge to our bodies' immune systems, which typically produce antibodies based on what surface structures are present.

Borrelia burgdorferi's **virulence** can also be attributed to the outer surface proteins. The *Borrelia burgdorferi* spirochete does not produce exotoxins, poisons that leave the cell, or endotoxins, which are poisons that remain in the cell and are released as the cell dies. The bacteria's virulence is associated with its ability to adhere to mammalian cells. This characteristic is a function of its outer surface proteins. The organism apparently produces few proteins itself and depends on its host(s), in true parasitic fashion, for nutrients.

GROWING THE ORGANISM

Robert Koch, one of the great microbiologists of the nineteenth and early twentieth centuries, devised a method for detecting and isolating a specific pathogen that causes a specific disease. The elements of this method have come to be known as Koch's Postulates, which can be applied to Lyme disease and can be used to isolate the pathogen, *Borrelia burgdorferi.*

- **Postulate #1:** *Borrelia burgdorferi* must be isolated from a diseased organism.

- **Postulate #2:** Bacteria are grown on culture media to produce a *Borrelia burgdorferia* pure (one species) culture.

- **Postulate #3:** Bacteria from the pure culture are then injected into a laboratory animal; usually white mice are used. Diseased mice show signs of both arthritis and cardiac disease.

- **Postulate #4:** *Borrelia burgdorferi* is then isolated from the infected laboratory animal and grown in a pure culture.

Culture media, nutrient material usually poured into a test tube or Petri plate, must be specifically made for a microorganism. For example, microbes each have their own nutrient requirements. Alan G. Barbour devised a medium for culturing *Borrelia burgdorferi*. Barbour further developed a medium created by Herbert Stoenner and Richard Kelly. This media is now called BSK media.

RESERVOIR HOSTS

Wildlife such as the raccoon, eastern chipmunk, meadow vole, woodland jumping mouse, cottontail rabbit, white-footed mouse, and a type of bird called the veery, are all known reservoir hosts—places where the bacteria *Borrelia burgdorferi* live and reproduce. The host can vary by region. The white-footed mouse, for example, is thought to be the main reservoir host for Connecticut, Long Island, and the Midwest. In California and Oregon, however, the dusky-footed wood rat hosts the bacteria. Horses and dogs are known to be infected with *Borrelia burgdorferi,* but do not function as reservoirs from which the infection may be passed on to ticks and humans.

HUMAN HOSTS AND SYMPTOMS

As the case studies in Chapter 1 showed, *Borrelia burgdorferi* does not generate the same exact symptoms in a specific linear fashion. However, its introduction and dissemination through the human body has been characterized in three stages.

The first stage in most early Lyme disease patients includes flu-like symptoms. Then, symptoms of malaise, fatigue, headaches, chills, fever, sore throat, dry cough, nausea, swollen lymph glands, and neck and back pain can follow in any order. At this stage, the spirochete is localized in the skin. Erythema migrans (expanding red rash), particularly in the lower extremities, can also occur.

The presence and/or absence and timing of the expanding red rash often causes confusion. It can appear any time during the first month after the bite. The rash usually has a red border with a hard, pale center, and a bull's-eye pattern that starts at the site of the tick bite and can expand up to 46 centimeters in diameter. Most patients, around 80%, exhibit this red rash, but a fair proportion of patients never exhibit the rash. Infection can exist whether or not the rash is present.

Like any parasite, the Lyme disease spirochete harms its human host. It gets nutrients from our bodies to live. Its outer cell envelope lipoproteins also stimulate our cells to produce cytokines, which are chemical messengers. These chemicals cause the blood vessels to dilate, thereby releasing blood (including white blood cells) to the infected area. This response is the body's way of preventing the bacteria from spreading. A consequence of this reaction is the red rash.

The second, or disseminated, stage of Lyme disease usually occurs within several weeks after the host has been inoculated with the bacteria. During this time the spirochete may spread to many organs and other sites of the body. Secondary rashes may appear. Pain can be experienced in joints, tendons, and muscles (Figure 3.4). Meningitis, Bell's palsy (a facial paralysis), and general nervous system involvement can occur.

MOTHER TO FETUS?

The placenta, a temporary organ that envelopes the developing fetus, serves to exchange nutrients and wastes between the blood of the mother and fetus. Bacteria, especially spirochetes, can also travel from mother to fetus through the placenta.

In one study, *Borrelia* was discovered during the first three months of pregnancy in 19 women. All were treated with antibiotics. Abnormalities occurred in five of the children. However, because the abnormalities were so varied, none could be directly linked to Lyme disease. Thus, congenital abnormalities associated with Lyme disease are considered possible, but rare.

Prevalence Rates of Clinical Manifestations of Lyme Borreliosis in Different Areas

	Skin	Nervous System	Joints	Heart
United States	76%	11%	46%	4%
Northern Europe	60%	33%	7%	1%
Southern Europe	44%	29%	21%	6%
Italy	54%	21%	30%	2%

Figure 3.4 Lyme disease can cause many different symptoms. Some of the most frequent symptoms of Lyme disease include skin rashes, joint and heart problems, and nervous system ailments. The prevalence rates for each type of symptom, for the United States, northern Europe, southern Europe, and Italy are shown here.

Also within several weeks, *Borrelia burgdorferi* can travel to the heart, where it impedes proper blood flow between heart chambers, a condition known as atrioventricular blockage. Myopericarditis, an inflammation of the muscle and membranes of the heart, can also occur. In rare cases, pancarditis, an inflammation of all the structures of the heart, develops and can be fatal.

During late Lyme disease, or stage three, patients can exhibit many of the problems seen in stage two, except that now these problems have become chronic. These can occur in the second and third year of the disease. A swelling of the brain and **dementia** may also occur. About 20% of patients who do not receive antibiotic treatment exhibit neurological complications. While these symptoms may take years to develop, some patients become symptomatic in a matter of weeks. To make diagnosis even more difficult for physicians, some patients' first and only indicator of Lyme disease is arthritis.

4

The Tick

This small vile creature [the tick] may, in the future, cause the inhabitants of the land [the present-day United States] great damage unless a method is discovered which will prevent it from increasing at such a shocking rate.

—Peter Kalm (late 1700s)

Lyme disease is a zoonosis—that is, a disease that affects humans and domesticated animals and that is carried and maintained in wildlife. In much of the United States, the carrier (or vector) that transmits the bacteria to humans is the black-legged tick (*Ixodes scapularis*), sometimes called a deer tick. The western black-legged tick (*Ixodes pacificus*) is the vector on the West Coast.

MYTHS

Along with other members of the **arachnid** family, ticks seem to hold a special fascination for people. As a consequence, myths involving ticks abound, including that ticks can jump great distances or can burst after overfeeding on blood. These myths even generated a cartoon superhero that had super-human strength and threatened to suck the blood of his enemies through a plastic straw. In reality, ticks have three blood meals in their entire lifetime.

TAXONOMY

Lyme disease was first described in the United States. It is the number one vector-borne disease, as well as the most common tick-borne and arthropod-borne disease in the United States. Although malaria, which

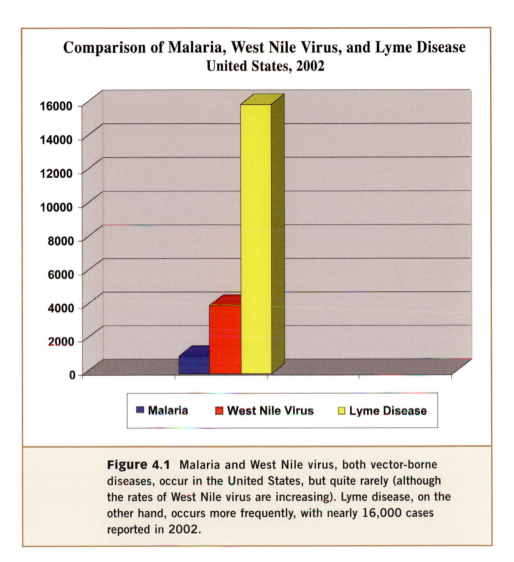

Comparison of Malaria, West Nile Virus, and Lyme Disease United States, 2002

Figure 4.1 Malaria and West Nile virus, both vector-borne diseases, occur in the United States, but quite rarely (although the rates of West Nile virus are increasing). Lyme disease, on the other hand, occurs more frequently, with nearly 16,000 cases reported in 2002.

is spread by mosquitoes, is the most common vector-borne disease in the world, there are only about 1,000 cases of malaria reported annually in the United States. The only **emerging** mosquito-borne disease in the United States is West Nile virus, but only 3,893 total cases have been reported as of February 2003. There are more than 15,000 Lyme disease cases reported each year (Figure 4.1).

Arthropods, one phylum of the animal kingdom, are organisms with hard exoskeletons, jointed appendages, and, for the most part, segmented bodies. Insects such as fleas and mosquitoes; and arachnids such as spiders, ticks, and mites are all arthropods. Ticks and mites are unique in that they lack segmented bodies. There are over 850 tick species worldwide, of which 100 are known disease vectors. In 1997, there were 400 cases of Rocky Mountain spotted fever, also a tick-borne illness, making Lyme disease both the most common tick-borne and arthropod-borne disease in the United States.

ANATOMY

Charles Darwin (1809–1882), the father of evolutionary theory and modern biology, used everything from beetles to fungi and even coral to exemplify his theory of natural selection. The essence of Darwin's theory of evolution is that the fittest survive. In other words, those organisms better adapted to their environment go on to reproduce successfully. Darwin could just as easily have used ticks to exemplify **fitness**. A quick glance at the anatomy of an *Ixodes scapularis* tick shows an organism with anatomical structures well adapted to its place in nature. The niche or role of sucking blood was filled by ticks, and natural selection has honed their anatomy very efficiently to the task.

The gnathosoma, or front structure, of an *Ixodes scapularis* tick is well suited for its hermatophagus (blood sucking) niche. The hypostone portion resembles a chain saw with a shark's curved teeth. There is a tube running the length of the hypostone that functions as a "straw," which the tick uses to suck the blood of its host. The long rigid pedipalps function to anchor the tick to its **host** (Figure 4.2).

There is considerable sexual dimorphism, or difference, between the male and female black-legged ticks. Unlike in many other animal species, female ticks are larger than males, and there is considerable debate about the reasons for this size

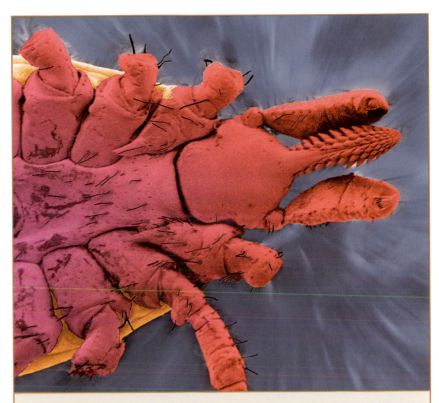

Figure 4.2 This image shows the anterior portion of a tick and its "toothed" hypostone. The pedipalps, which help the tick attach to its host, are located along each side of the hypostone. The tick sucks blood from its host through the hypostone.

difference. The females have a reddish brown body, and the males are completely dark brown.

Ticks, as members of the arachnid group of arthropods, have four pairs of legs, in contrast to insects, which have three pairs. During its larval stage, *Ixodes scapularis* has only three pairs of legs, which can be a source of confusion.

LIFE CYCLE

After laying around 2,000 eggs, usually in the spring, the female tick dies. The larvae hatch about one month later. They are very

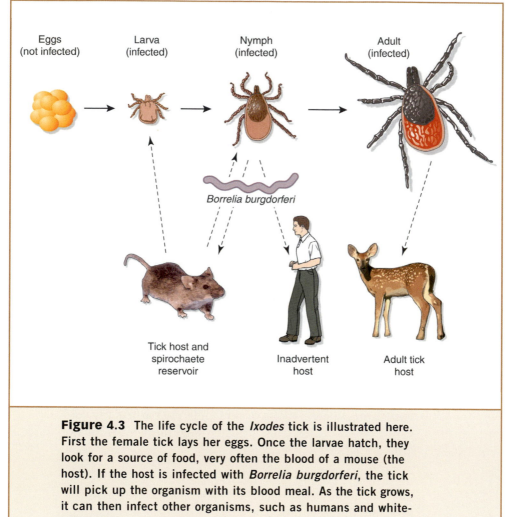

Eggs   Larva   Nymph   Adult
(not infected)   (infected)   (infected)   (infected)

Borrelia burgdorferi

Tick host and
spirochaete   Inadvertent   Adult tick
reservoir   host   host

Figure 4.3 The life cycle of the *Ixodes* tick is illustrated here.
First the female tick lays her eggs. Once the larvae hatch, they
look for a source of food, very often the blood of a mouse (the
host). If the host is infected with *Borrelia burgdorferi*, the tick
will pick up the organism with its blood meal. As the tick grows,
it can then infect other organisms, such as humans and white-
tailed deer.

small, almost invisible to the naked eye. After hatching, they
search for a blood source. Attaching to a host for a two-day
period, the larvae feed only once during this stage. The ticks
could potentially become infected with the bacteria at this
point. Larvae become dormant through the next winter,
completing their first year of life (Figure 4.3).

During the second spring of their lives, larvae molt into the nymphal stage of development. Nymphs also attach to a host. In New England, the white-footed mouse often plays this role. The ticks may become infected with *Borrelia burgdorferi* at this stage if the mouse is infected with the bacteria. The ticks attach for up to 3 to 4 days. The ultimate opportunists, ticks will attach to whatever passes their way. Many studies suggest that ticks in the nymphal stage tend to attach to humans. It is important to keep in mind that ticks can function as infectious agents at any stage of their life cycle. They molt into adults by the end of their second summer.

Adult black-legged ticks, which are about 1.5 millimeters wide (males), search for a specific host, more specific than at any other stage of their life cycle. White tailed deer are by far their favorite blood meal at this stage of development. Male and female ticks mate quite often while still on the deer. After mating, the male dies and the female lives through the winter, feeding on the deer to nourish her eggs. The female lays her eggs in the third spring and then dies (Figure 4.4).

It is common to hear meteorologists discuss tick survivorship during winter storms or years that are particularly cold and icy. These predictions usually imply dire effects on the tick populations in the area due to the severe weather. From the eggs to adults, ticks are wonderfully adapted to survive under ice and snow. In fact, they tend to be protected in this way from their predators (e.g., birds).

PHYSIOLOGY OF THE BITE

A tick's bite is painless, an important feature because the tick must remain attached, and therefore undetected, for many hours or even days to consume enough blood and nutrients to last it for months. If the bite caused an irritation, the tick might be removed by the host organism. Secretions from the tick's salivary glands dilate the capillaries in the host's

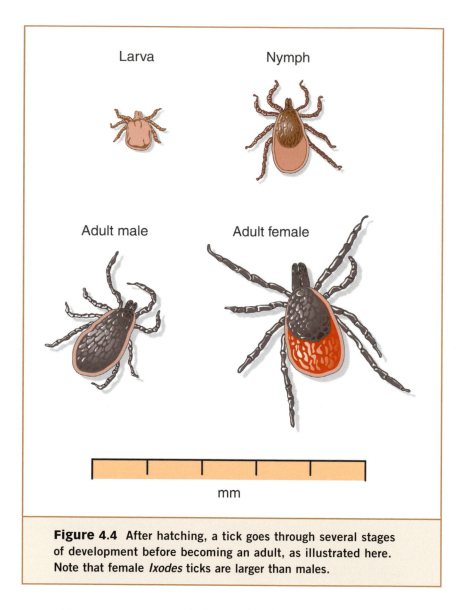

Larva

Nymph

Adult male

Adult female

mm

Figure 4.4 After hatching, a tick goes through several stages of development before becoming an adult, as illustrated here. Note that female *Ixodes* ticks are larger than males.

skin to prevent coagulation and enhance blood flow. The tick sucks blood through the hypostone into its intestine. Here, nutrients are absorbed into its cells, where they are metabolized for energy. The months between blood meals make this a necessity.

Once a tick has become infected with *Borrelia burgdorferi* after a blood meal, two scenarios may occur. Once in the intestine, the spirochetes can pass through the intestinal cells into the tick's body cavity. Some bacteria can make their way to the salivary glands and infect with the next attachment. Or, some bacteria may remain in the intestine in a semiquiescent or semi-inactive state. After the next bite or attachment and intake of blood, the bacteria are stimulated to divide by the increase in temperature and nutrients. Once the tick is thoroughly engorged, it regurgitates into the host, thus infecting it with *Borrelia burgdorferi*.

THE NAME GAME

Lyme disease is inextricably linked to ticks. At one point in the history of this relatively new disease, it became a question of which type of tick was responsible for Lyme disease.

In the late 1970s, one of Allen Steere's patients brought a tick to him around the time Steere was reading a European text connecting red rashes with ticks. The tick was identified as *Ixodes scapularis*, quite common in the areas under investigation.

About this time, Andrew Spielman of Harvard University found what he believed were new characteristics in this particular Ixodid tick. He named the tick *Ixodes dammini* after a famous Harvard pathologist, Gustave Dammin. By 1977, *Ixodes dammini* was viewed as the etiological or infectious agent for Lyme disease. The matter appeared to be settled.

By the early 1990s, research scientists at the Connecticut Agricultural Experiment Station published observations that showed the deer tick to be the common *Ixodes scapularis*. They saw no morphological evidence to denote a separate and new species. A kind of taxonomical tug of war between Harvard and the Agricultural Center ensued. The result was that the black-legged tick (or deer tick) was once again anointed *Ixodes scapularis*.

OTHER TICK-BORNE DISEASES

Although other diseases are carried by ticks, two diseases in particular are occasionally mentioned in the Lyme disease literature. Rocky Mountain spotted fever was the most common tick-borne disease in the United States before the discovery of Lyme disease. It is carried by a tick of the *Dermacentor* and *Amblyomma* genera, which carry the etiological agent *Rickettsia rickettsii*. In 1997, there were 400 cases reported, mostly in the southeastern and Atlantic Coast states. The disease is characterized by a rash that begins with spots, as well as a high fever.

Another illness associated with *Amblyomma americanum* is Southern tick-associated rash. This tick has a white dot on its back side, thus the common name "lone star" tick. The bacteria detected in this tick are called *Borrelia lonestari*. Known in southeastern and south-central states, it causes a Lyme disease-like expanding red rash.

Although *Ixodes scapularis* is widely known to carry Lyme disease, it also carries other diseases. Babesiosis, transmitted by *Ixodes scapularis*, is sometimes referred to as a companion to Lyme disease. It is not, however, bacterial. It is caused by a **protist**, *Babesia microti*, which resembles the malaria parasite and generates similar symptoms—headache, fatigue, fever, and chills. This parasite, like its malaria counterpart, also invades and destroys red blood cells, resulting in a lower red blood cell count.

Human granulocytic ehrlichiosis is caused by bacteria of the genus *Ehrlichia*. It is transmitted by Ixodid ticks, both *Ixodes scapularis* and *Ixodes pacificus*, but can also be transmitted by the dog tick, *Dermacentor variabilis*. This disease affects the human white blood cells called granulocytes, and causes a low white blood cell count, headache, malaise, and fever. It can also cause liver disease.

Ixodes scapularis and four other ticks can cause tick paralysis. This condition is more widespread among cows and sheep, although rare cases among humans have been reported. This malady is also distinct from the others as it involves a **neurotoxin**. As egg-laden or gravid female ticks become engorged, a neurotoxin is generated from their salivary glands. Data have shown that the tick must be attached for at least 5 to 7 days for infection to occur. Because ticks are usually discovered when they are engorged, humans are rarely afflicted with this disease. Early symptoms include fatigue, numbness of the legs, and considerable muscle pain. If the tick is not removed, numbness travels to the upper extremities and is followed by tongue and facial paralysis. Up to 12% of untreated cases result in death.

5

Ecology

If we were to grasp the true nature of nature—if we could comprehend the real meaning of evolution—then we would envision a world in which every living plant, insect, and animal species is changing at every instant, in response to every other living plant, insect, and animal.

—*Prey*, Michael Crichton

HABITAT

To learn more about Lyme disease, scientists have identified the **preferred habitat** of *Ixodes scapularis*, the black-legged ticks. Scientists have searched for ticks in many different habitats. To do this, they use a procedure known as a "tick drag," which involves attaching a piece of corduroy or flannel cloth to a long stick or pole. This apparatus is then dragged through the study area. Ticks will cling to the fabric and can be counted and preserved for further study (Figure 5.1).

"Edge habitat" is the favored habitat for ticks. These are typical transitional zones between one area and another. One example of edge habitat is the area of small shrubs and seedlings found near a picnic area by the sandy beach of a lake or pond. This edge habitat is usually adjacent to woodlands or forest.

Ticks prefer this habitat for two reasons. First, ticks cannot jump or fly. They can only attach to objects, such as leaves or grass. Second, ticks are most likely to encounter their desired hosts, such as white-footed mice or white-tailed deer, in this habitat. As the host moves through the habitat, it comes in contact with many grass blades, shrubs, and seedling

Figure 5.1 Shown here is a tick drag, which is one method used for sampling tick abundance in a particular habitat. A piece of corduroy or flannel cloth is attached to a long pole. The cloth is dragged through a sampling area, and ticks, which will attach to the cloth, can be removed for study later.

twigs where ticks await. During this process, the animal hosts are both dropping off and picking up deer ticks in these transitional zones.

DEER

Although many mammals play host to the black-legged tick, none supports more ticks per animal than do deer. Studies have shown that deer are crucial to the adult stage of *Ixodes scapularis*. Deer, although they give the tick a temporary home and a ready supply of blood, are not a **reservoir** for the *Borrelia burgdorferi*, the causative agent of Lyme disease (Figure 5.2).

During the colonial period, settlers cleared forest land for agriculture. This led to a decreased number of deer in the area, as the forest was their home. Throughout the twentieth century, the deer population has recovered from this loss. The United States' deer population has grown from about 500,000 at the turn of the twentieth century to 30 million today. In 1900, only

GLOBAL WARMING AND LYME DISEASE

Global warming has been a major issue in the scientific community. Scenarios usually include the problem of rising temperatures, leading to major flooding of coastal cities, expanding deserts, and diminishing agricultural output. Global warming not only affects temperatures; it also affects disease patterns.

The main culprit is carbon dioxide, which traps the radiant energy of the sun in what is usually referred to as the greenhouse effect. Carbon dioxide from human activity such as industry and automobiles has increased by 25% over the last 200 years, and is continuing to rise. Over 50% of this increase has occurred since 1950. In 2002, an entire island in the Pacific had to be abandoned and its inhabitants relocated because of rising seawaters.

Increasing global temperatures could also affect the population of white-tailed deer. A general warming would lead to an expansion of the deciduous and mixed conifer forests of New England, Wisconsin, and Canada. Because these forests are the preferred habitat of deer, this could mean a considerable increase in Lyme disease cases north of the border. Also, warming in temperate areas would mean that people would be outdoors for longer periods during the year, a factor which could also lead to more Lyme disease cases.

Figure 5.2 Deer often serve as a host for the adult ticks that carry Lyme disease. Research has shown a correlation between the number of deer in an area and the number of reported Lyme disease cases. Some states are taking measures to reduce increasing deer populations.

12 deer were sighted in Connecticut, although the method of counting was crude compared to the aerial census procedure used today. By the winter of 1987–1988, the Connecticut Department of Environmental Protection (DEP) estimated the state's deer population at 31,000. In the winter of 1999–2000, a DEP census revealed 76,000 deer in the state. With this data, it is easy to understand how, during the middle to latter part of the twentieth century, infected ticks were transported from islands off the mainland of Connecticut and found suitable hosts.

The increase in the deer population alone, however, does not explain the perfusion of Lyme disease cases. People have to come in contact with areas that deer frequent. Changing modes of transportation and housing throughout the twentieth century are important factors. With the waning of the nation's mass transportation system came an emphasis on automobile travel. This was coupled with increased road building and a housing pattern that radiated from urban areas. This phenomenon, aptly called sprawl, brought people in closer contact with the fauna involved in the **pathogenesis** of Lyme disease.

BIOGEOGRAPHY

Some scientists have suggested that the distribution of Lyme disease cases positively correlates to states with large deer populations. The majority of Lyme disease cases are reported in Connecticut, Massachusetts, Rhode Island, New York, New Jersey, Pennsylvania, Minnesota, and Wisconsin—states that have large deer populations. There are, however, states with large deer populations that do not exhibit this correlation, particularly southern states (Figure 5.3).

Biogeography, the study of the distribution of fauna and flora over the earth, has shown that ticks will attach to the first organism they contact. For example, reptiles are abundant in Maryland and other southern states. The southern black-legged tick, *Ixodes scapularis*, comes in contact with many lizards and feeds on them. The lizards do not appear to be infected with *Borrelia burgdorferi* and, therefore, do not infect the ticks. This greatly reduces the number of ticks feeding on mice because there is an ample supply of lizard hosts. This, in turn, greatly reduces the number of ticks carrying the bacteria and reduces the number of cases of Lyme disease, even where large populations of deer exist. This phenomenon also applies to the black-legged tick, *Ixodes pacificus*, which is a capable vector of Lyme disease in California and Oregon, but which feeds on the many lizards in that region, rather than mice and other rodents. *Ixodes ricinus*, the sheep tick, is the vector for Lyme disease in Europe and Asia. (For more on the subject, see "Lyme Disease, Biodiversity, and the Dilution Effect," page 50.)

INTERRELATIONSHIPS BETWEEN HOST, HABITAT, AND DISEASE

The habitat, host, and life cycle of the deer tick tell us about the component parts of Lyme disease. What they do not

LYME DISEASE. Reported cases by county — United States, 2001

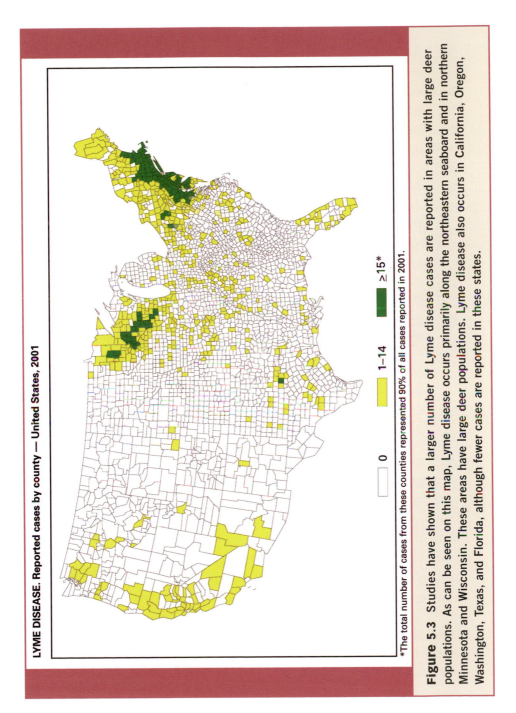

0   1–14   ≥15*

*The total number of cases from these counties represented 90% of all cases reported in 2001.

Figure 5.3   Studies have shown that a larger number of Lyme disease cases are reported in areas with large deer populations. As can be seen on this map, Lyme disease occurs primarily along the northeastern seaboard and in northern Minnesota and Wisconsin. These areas have large deer populations. Lyme disease also occurs in California, Oregon, Washington, Texas, and Florida, although fewer cases are reported in these states.

LYME DISEASE, BIODIVERSITY, AND THE DILUTION EFFECT

Biodiversity appears easy to define and even easier to comprehend. It is most often explained as the array of different organisms in a given habitat. However, it can also be applied at the genetic level, at the species level, and in other taxonomic categories. It can even refer to the variety of habitats and communities in a given area. Less acknowledged, however, is the role of biodiversity in ecosystem health, including its impact on humans.

A typical scenario that impacts the biodiversity of an area is urban/suburban sprawl. The first impact is on larger animals, quite often coyotes and fox, mammals that need a considerable area in which to range. As these predators become more scarce, animals that these **omnivores** may prey on, such as raccoons, tend to increase. Raccoons prey on song birds' nest sites, dessimating their eggs and young, thus hurting the bird diversity of the area. Soon blackbirds and other edge species move in to fill the niches left by the variety of song birds that no longer populate the area.

How does biodiversity relate to Lyme disease? Sprawl impacts natural areas where owls and other birds of prey live. As these predators are driven out, the rodent population rises. In New England, for example, this includes white-footed mice, which are the major reservoir host for the bacteria causing Lyme disease. Other mammals and birds driven out may only be a small part of Lyme pathogenesis or not part of it at all.

When biodiversity is strong, different scenarios come into play. More species diversity means that ticks have more choices while questing and, therefore, are more apt to attach to hosts that are not reservoirs for Lyme disease. In this way, fewer ticks pick up the bacteria and fewer are able to pass on the infectious agent to humans. Ecologists call this the dilution effect. It is just one of the many reasons why biodiversity is crucial to ecosystem health, and to our health, as we are part of these very same ecosystems.

tell us is how the parts fit together. How do they interact in the environment?

The interaction of the component parts may help us understand the ebb and flow of Lyme disease on a year-by-year basis. Ecologists Dr. Richard S. Ostfeld and Dr. Clive G. Jones of the Institute of Ecosystem Studies in Millbrook, New York, looked closely at the cycle of events in northeastern forests. They knew that key players in the life cycle of the deer tick, *Ixodes scapularis*, were dependent on the forest for food. Important questions included which nutrients were necessary and exactly how fluctuation in these nutrients would impact ticks and Lyme disease outbreaks.

The study sites included the Mary Flagler Cary Arboretum at the Institute at Millbrook and forests at the Mountain Lake Biological Station in Virginia. Dr. Jerry O. Wolff, a biologist at Oregon State University, selected the latter site due to the 14-year study of mouse populations in that area.

The focus of the study was a common forest floor food—acorns. The scientists knew the importance of this key element, what they call forest mast, for sustaining the forests' most common rodent inhabitant, the white-footed mouse. They also studied the interplay with deer, ticks, and gypsy moths. The moths were the only nonindigenous species studied.

The scientists knew that acorn production changed each year. Some years, many acorns were produced. Other years, acorn production decreased. They selected for study peak acorn production years of 1980, 1985, 1988, and 1989 in Virginia, and 1991 and 1994 in New York.

Using a capture-and-release system, the scientists found that white-footed mice populations increased the summer after acorn production ("mast") increased. Apparently, the bumper crop of acorns enabled the female mice to reproduce and sustain large numbers of offspring. Accordingly, as acorn production dropped that year, so did the population

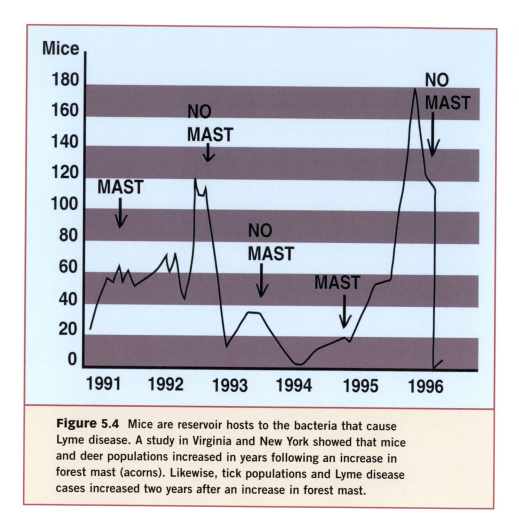

Figure 5.4 Mice are reservoir hosts to the bacteria that cause Lyme disease. A study in Virginia and New York showed that mice and deer populations increased in years following an increase in forest mast (acorns). Likewise, tick populations and Lyme disease cases increased two years after an increase in forest mast.

of mice (Figure 5.4). They found that deer populations also increased after the increase in acorns. They also found that, in the years following bumper crops of acorns, tick populations increased. Specifically, two years after acorns increased, the tick population increased. This two-year lag was also followed by an increase in reported Lyme disease cases. The forest mast had a direct impact on the key fauna (or animals) in the tick life cycle and thus on the subsequent accidental human hosts.

One last piece of the ecological puzzle was the role of the gypsy moth. These were what scientists call an **ecological introduction**. Accidentally released into forests of the Americas, they have done great harm, mainly denuding trees of their leaves. Mice feed on gypsy moth pupae, the third stage in their maturation process. Studying one year in which the mouse population was moderately high, they found that all gypsy moth pupae were eaten in eight days. The next year, when the mouse population plummeted, the moths reached adulthood. Interestingly, weather had no significant impact on the fauna studied. The study demonstrated the connection between ecosystem health and human health.

6

Lyme Disease Epidemiology

Epidemiology at any given time is something more than the total of its established facts. It includes their orderly arrangement into chains of inference which extend more or less beyond the bounds of direct observation. Such of these chains as are well and truly laid guide investigation to the facts of the future.

—Wade Hampton Frost, in the introduction to John Snow's *Snow on Cholera*

EPIDEMIOLOGY

The science and methods of epidemiology took center stage in the discovery of Lyme disease. Epidemiology is about numbers. It is the study of the incidence, transmission, and distribution of disease. It continues to play an important role in monitoring Lyme disease throughout the world. When a solution to the spread of Lyme disease is implemented, such as vaccination or genetic engineering, epidemiologists will be called upon to determine the solution's effectiveness.

THE WORLD SCENE

North America is not the only area of the world to report cases of Lyme disease. All continents except Antarctica have reported evidence of Lyme infection. These data range from positive blood cultures to clinical descriptions, to positive antibody tests, to birds carrying infected ticks. However, Lyme disease appears restricted to temperate zones. Tropical

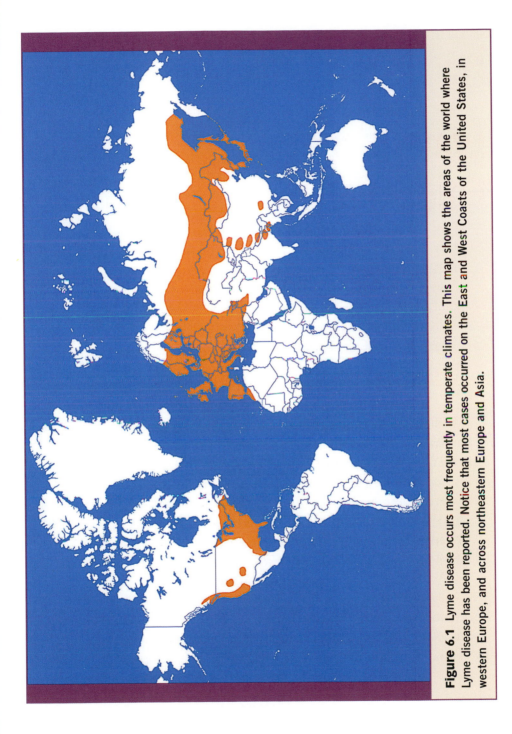

Figure 6.1 Lyme disease occurs most frequently in temperate climates. This map shows the areas of the world where Lyme disease has been reported. Notice that most cases occurred on the East and West Coasts of the United States, in western Europe, and across northeastern Europe and Asia.

and desert areas do not show evidence of Lyme disease infection. Most incidences of the disease occur in the United States (East and West Coasts) and in northern Europe and Asia (Figure 6.1).

THE UNITED STATES

The data presented here are for the entire United States. There are a number of important statistical approaches by which to collect and evaluate epidemiological data that should be kept in mind. Although current data are always important, epidemiologists like to use data that are older because they have been analyzed more, and hence tend to be more accurate. Thus, the following data table in Figure 6.2a from the Centers for Disease Control and Prevention (CDC) for the United States, by state and by region, ranges from 1990 to 1999. Figure 6.2b presents the data for Connecticut, where Lyme disease is especially prevalent.

What is most important, from an epidemiological standpoint, is to arrive at a standard definition for Lyme disease that all states and counties can use. With common disease criteria, the data collected are more accurate. The CDC's clinical case definition for Lyme disease is as follows: (1) either erythema migrans (EM) or at least one late musculoskeletal or cardiovascular manifestation (problems with the muscular or cardiovascular systems) must be present; and (2) there needs to be a laboratory confirmation of infection, including isolation of *Borrelia burgdorferi* from clinical specimen, antibody detection in serum or cerebral spinal fluid, or a sensitive enzyme immunoassay or immunofluorescence antibody test, followed by a Western blot, which positively identifies *Borrelia burgdorferi* in the patient's system.

Based on this definition, Lyme disease has been reported in every state except Montana. With more than 145,000 cases reported since 1982, it has become the most common vector-borne disease in the United States, comprising more than 95% of all vector-borne illnesses in the United States (see Chapter 4).

Epidemiologists commonly represent their data on a per

Lyme Disease Cases Reported to CDC by State Health Departments, 1990–1999

STATE	Region	1990	1991	1992	1993	1994	1995	1996	1997	1998	1999	TOTAL	1995 POP	INC 98	INC 99	ANN INC
ALABAMA	ESC	33	13	10	4	6	12	9	11	24	20	142	4.246	0.57	0.47	0.33
ALASKA	PAC	0	0	0	0	0	0	0	2	1	0	3	0.603	0.17	0.00	0.05
ARIZONA	MT	0	1	0	0	0	1	0	4	1	3	10	4.305	0.02	0.07	0.02
ARKANSAS	WSC	22	31	20	8	15	11	27	27	8	7	176	2.485	0.32	0.28	0.71
CALIFORNIA	PAC	345	265	231	134	68	84	64	154	135	139	1619	31.565	0.43	0.44	0.51
COLORADO	MT	0	1	0	0	1	0	0	0	0	3	5	3.748	0.00	0.08	0.01
CONNECTICUT	NE	704	1192	1760	1350	2030	1548	3104	2297	3434	3215	20634	3.271	104.99	98.30	63.09
DELAWARE	SA	54	73	219	143	106	56	173	109	77	167	1177	0.717	10.74	23.29	16.41
DC	SA	5	5	3	2	9	3	3	10	8	6	54	0.555	1.44	1.08	0.97
FLORIDA	SA	7	35	24	30	28	17	55	56	71	59	382	14.184	0.50	0.42	0.27
GEORGIA	SA	161	25	48	44	127	14	1	9	5	0	434	7.209	0.07	0.00	0.60
HAWAII	PAC	2	0	2	1	0	0	1	0	0	0	6	1.179	0.00	0.00	0.05
IDAHO	MT	1	2	2	2	3	0	2	4	7	3	26	1.166	0.60	0.26	0.22
ILLINOIS	ENC	30	51	41	19	24	18	10	13	14	17	237	11.790	0.12	0.14	0.20
INDIANA	ENC	15	16	22	32	19	19	32	33	39	21	248	5.797	0.67	0.36	0.43
IOWA	WNC	16	22	33	8	17	16	19	8	27	24	190	2.843	0.95	0.84	0.67
KANSAS	WNC	14	22	18	54	17	23	36	4	13	16	217	2.564	0.51	0.62	0.85
KENTUCKY	ESC	18	44	28	16	24	16	26	20	27	19	238	3.857	0.70	0.49	0.62
LOUISIANA	WSC	3	6	7	3	4	9	9	13	15	9	78	4.338	0.35	0.21	0.18
MAINE	NE	9	15	16	18	33	45	63	34	78	41	352	1.239	6.30	3.31	2.84
MARYLAND	SA	238	282	183	180	341	454	447	494	659	899	4177	2.039	13.08	17.84	8.29
MASSACHUSETTS	NE	117	265	223	148	247	189	321	291	699	787	3287	6.071	11.51	12.96	5.41
MICHIGAN	ENC	134	46	35	23	33	5	28	27	17	11	359	9.538	0.18	0.12	0.38
MINNESOTA	WNC	70	84	197	141	208	208	251	256	261	283	1959	4.615	5.66	6.13	4.25
MISSISSIPPI	ESC	7	8	0	0	0	17	24	27	17	4	104	2.696	0.63	0.15	0.39
MISSOURI	WNC	205	207	150	108	102	53	52	28	12	72	989	5.319	0.23	1.35	1.86
MONTANA	MT	0	0	0	0	0	0	0	0	0	0	0	0.870	0.00	0.00	0.00
NEBRASKA	WNC	0	25	22	6	3	6	5	2	4	11	84	1.639	0.24	0.67	0.51
NEVADA	MT	2	5	1	5	1	6	2	2	6	2	32	1.533	0.39	0.13	0.21
NEW HAMPSHIRE	NE	4	38	44	15	30	28	47	39	45	27	317	1.148	3.92	2.35	2.76
NEW JERSEY	MA	1074	915	688	786	1533	1703	2190	2041	1911	1719	14560	7.950	24.04	21.62	18.32
NEW MEXICO	MT	0	3	2	2	5	1	1	1	4	1	20	1.690	0.24	0.06	0.12
NEW YORK	MA	3244	3944	3448	2818	5200	4438	5301	3327	4640	4402	40762	18.191	25.51	24.20	22.41
NORTH CAROLINA	SA	87	73	67	86	77	84	66	34	63	74	711	7.202	0.87	1.03	0.99
NORTH DAKOTA	WNC	3	2	1	2	0	0	2	0	0	1	11	0.642	0.00	0.16	0.17
OHIO	ENC	36	112	32	30	45	30	32	40	47	47	451	11.134	0.42	0.42	0.41
OKLAHOMA	WSC	13	29	27	19	99	63	42	45	13	8	358	3.284	0.40	0.24	1.09
OREGON	PAC	11	5	13	8	6	20	19	20	21	15	138	3.149	0.67	0.48	0.44
PENNSYLVANIA	MA	553	718	1173	1085	1438	1562	2814	2188	2760	2781	17072	12.060	22.88	23.06	14.16
RHODE ISLAND	NE	101	142	275	272	471	345	534	442	789	546	3917	0.992	79.56	55.06	39.50
SOUTH CAROLINA	SA	7	10	2	9	7	17	9	3	8	6	78	3.667	0.22	0.16	0.21
SOUTH DAKOTA	WNC	2	1	1	0	0	0	0	1	0	0	5	0.730	0.00	0.00	0.07
TENNESSEE	ESC	28	35	31	20	13	28	24	45	47	59	330	5.247	0.90	1.12	0.63
TEXAS	WSC	44	57	113	48	56	77	97	60	32	72	656	18.801	0.17	0.38	0.35
UTAH	MT	1	2	6	2	3	1	1	1	0	2	19	1.958	0.00	0.10	0.10
VERMONT	NE	11	7	9	12	16	9	26	8	11	26	135	0.585	1.88	4.45	2.31
VIRGINIA	SA	129	151	123	95	131	55	57	67	73	122	1003	6.615	1.10	1.84	1.52
WASHINGTON	PAC	30	7	14	9	4	10	18	11	7	14	124	5.448	0.13	0.26	0.23
WEST VIRGINIA	SA	11	43	14	50	29	26	12	10	13	20	228	1.825	0.71	1.10	1.25
WISCONSIN	ENC	337	424	525	401	409	369	396	480	657	490	4488	5.122	12.83	9.57	8.76
WYOMING	MT	5	11	5	9	5	4	3	3	1	3	49	0.479	0.21	0.63	1.02
U.S. TOTAL		7943	9470	9908	8257	13043	11700	16455	12801	16801	16273	122651	262.889	6.39	6.19	4.67

*NOTE: Population is in millions; INC = incidence (cases) per 100,000 population;
ANN INC = mean annual incidence 1990-99; excludes 2 cases reported from Guam, one each in 1992 and 1998.

Figure 6.2a This chart displays the number of cases of Lyme disease per state, for the years 1990–1999. Notice that Connecticut, New Jersey, New York, and Pennsylvania have the highest rates for all 10 years.

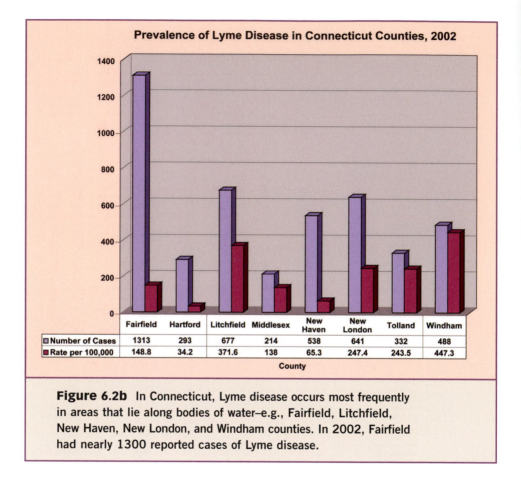

Prevalence of Lyme Disease in Connecticut Counties, 2002

	Fairfield	Hartford	Litchfield	Middlesex	New Haven	New London	Tolland	Windham
Number of Cases	1313	293	677	214	538	641	332	488
Rate per 100,000	148.8	34.2	371.6	138	65.3	247.4	243.5	447.3

County

Figure 6.2b In Connecticut, Lyme disease occurs most frequently in areas that lie along bodies of water–e.g., Fairfield, Litchfield, New Haven, New London, and Windham counties. In 2002, Fairfield had nearly 1300 reported cases of Lyme disease.

100,000 population basis. When this standard frame of reference is applied to Lyme disease, the result is an incidence of 5 cases per 100,000 people in the United States. As high as these figures are, some scientists feel it represents a considerable under-count. One statistical study estimated that the real number of cases at 1.5 to 2 million.

The incidence of cases per 100,000 (INC) makes it much easier to compare states having small populations with more populous states. A quick glance down the INC column for states, either 1998 or 1999, shows that Connecticut has the high-est incidence of Lyme disease in the United States (refer again to

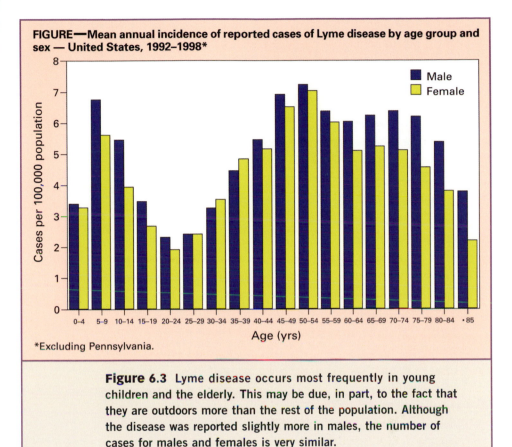

FIGURE—Mean annual incidence of reported cases of Lyme disease by age group and sex — United States, 1992–1998*

*Excluding Pennsylvania.

Figure 6.3 Lyme disease occurs most frequently in young children and the elderly. This may be due, in part, to the fact that they are outdoors more than the rest of the population. Although the disease was reported slightly more in males, the number of cases for males and females is very similar.

Figure 6.2a). As Lyme disease has a persistent presence in human populations in Connecticut, it is said to be endemic there.

STATISTICS BY AGE

The most vulnerable age groups for Lyme disease infection are the very young and the elderly (Figure 6.3). The very young, due to developing immune systems, and elderly, due to **compromised** immune systems, are generally at greater risk for disease. Also, because youngsters are more likely than adults to come in contact with the ground during play outdoors, they are particularly susceptible to tick bites. The senior population also tends to be more in contact with the environment perhaps due to the pursuit of gardening and other outdoor recreation activities, particularly after retirement.

Young adult and adult populations are generally not outdoors as much, being instead at school or work. This results in

TOO MANY CASES?

Education about an emerging disease is not just a problem for the community at large; it is also an awareness issue in the medical community itself. A gap often exists between the time a new infectious disease is reported in the medical literature and when its symptoms become familiar to local medical practitioners. Being in an endemic area and proximity to medical academic institutions are also factors that come into play.

Such has certainly been the case with Lyme disease, particularly given its propensity to mimic other diseases. This led some researchers to speculate that there are actually more cases of Lyme disease than are being reported. It was speculated that some people were intentionally reporting false cases of Lyme disease.

In December 2002, the *New York Times* exposed a group of New Jersey physicians who were treating what seemed to be an abnormally high number of Lyme disease patients. Apparently, the physicians were receiving a sizable payment for referring patients to a home intravenous (IV) antibiotic therapy company. Another example is a Connecticut physician who was connected to a similar company. When people who thought they had some Lyme disease symptoms called 1-800-TICKBITE, they would be referred to this doctor. The doctor, in turn, quite often referred these people back to the home infusion company that was responsible for the toll-free number. All profited from the referrals except the patients, who spent considerable sums of money on this expensive home therapy that did not cure their ailments.

a reduced opportunity for contact with the environment during day-to-day activities. Of course, adults who work outdoors are an exception. In Connecticut, three out of the seven employees in the Water Division of the Department of Environmental Protection contracted Lyme disease in the late 1980s.

Suburban sprawl is also a factor that has increased the likelihood of human contact with ticks. As recreational activities are played on fields in more suburban and rural areas, often bordering undeveloped land, the chance for young people to come in contact with edge habitat greatly increases. Because ticks favor these edge habitats, it is likely that humans playing in these areas will be more susceptible to tick bites.

STATISTICS BY MONTH

Lyme disease incidence is much higher during warmer months. Data indicate that the months of June and July have the highest incidence in Connecticut. This has as much to do with people being more active outdoors as it does with ticks searching for hosts. However, the incidence rates remain considerable into the fall. This may be due to a variety of seasonal activities such as fall crop harvests, increased hunting, and many activities associated with the changing colors of leaves such as hiking, camping, and photography.

7

The Tests and Treatments for Lyme Disease

Natural selection—working on host and pathogen alike—drives some devastating bargains.

—Gregory Cochran and Paul W. Ewald

DIAGNOSIS

The diagnosis of Lyme disease has confounded many medical professionals. The fact that the symptoms of Lyme disease are very similar to those of other diseases is just part of the challenge. Even if Lyme disease is suspected in a given patient, the quality of the diagnostic tests can still affect outcomes. For example, a false-negative test could leave a person with the debilitating effects of late Lyme disease for the rest of his or her life.

For some diseases, growing samples in culture media is one way to diagnose the disease. If the samples that are isolated from a sick patient match samples from known diseases, the diagnosis is fairly conclusive. However, Lyme disease is caused by a spirochete, and spirochetes are difficult to culture. For example, unlike *E. coli*, which produces three generations in an hour, spirochetes take much longer to reproduce. This delay would waste precious time for the patient, if treatment is eventually deemed necessary. Secondly, culturing would have to be done very early in the course of the disease, because in later stages the bacteria are difficult to locate as they penetrate deeper into body tissues. Even if a sample is taken at an early stage, it still may take weeks to grow to detectable levels. Culturing the Lyme bacteria is usually not done **clinically** but is reserved for research purposes.

Because culturing *Borrelia burgdorferi* is so difficult, other methods such as enzyme-linked immunosorbent assay (ELISA) tests, Western blots, and DNA probes are used to test for and diagnose Lyme disease.

ELISA TESTS

A serology (blood) test is the most common test for Lyme disease. The ELISA test is the technique used to recognize antibodies produced by the body in reaction to exposure to *Borrelia burgdorferi*. This process of our immune system is referred to as antibody-mediated immunity (AMI), also known as the **humoral** response.

As an ELISA test is a multistep process involving the layering of the patient's blood over specific antigens, followed by more layering of an antibody-enzyme over the antigen-antibody layers, it can be thought of as a "molecular sandwich" (Figure 7.1). A special plate containing multiple sample wells is used in this procedure. The surface of each well is coated with the proteins (antigens) of *Borrelia burgdorferi*. Blood serum is drawn from the patient and added to the well, and the wells are washed. If the patient's serum contains antibodies that were formed in response to exposure to *Borrelia burgdorferi*, the antibodies will recognize and attach to the *Borrelia burgdorferi* antigens present in the well. The antibodies are specific and will only attach to *Borrelia burgdorferi* antigens. Thus, if *Borrelia burgdorferi* antigens are not present, the antibodies will be washed away.

A second **antiglobulin** antibody is then added to the well. This antibody is attached to a special enzyme, such as horse-radish peroxidase, which changes color in response to a colorizing agent. However, this antibody will only attach if the previous antibodies are present in the well. The wells are then washed. A colorizing solution or substrate is added last to detect the enzyme. A positive test is indicated by a color change in the well. This change in color will occur only if the

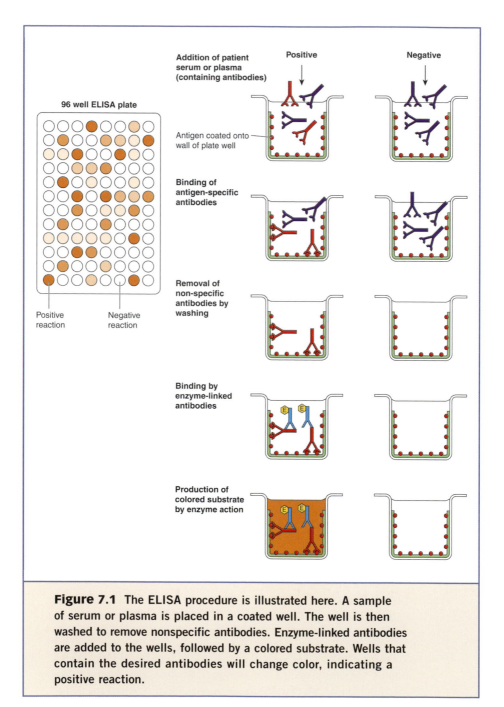

Figure 7.1 The ELISA procedure is illustrated here. A sample of serum or plasma is placed in a coated well. The well is then washed to remove nonspecific antibodies. Enzyme-linked antibodies are added to the wells, followed by a colored substrate. Wells that contain the desired antibodies will change color, indicating a positive reaction.

antigen-antibody–antibody-enzyme molecular sandwich is intact. A negative test is colorless, which indicates that bonding did not occur and therefore antibodies to *Borrelia burgdorferi* are not present.

The problems with this test are considerable. False negatives occur when the test is performed too early in the pathogenesis of the disease. This occurs, for example, when *Borrelia burgdorferi* is present, but there has not been enough time for the body to build up detectable blood antibody levels. False positives can also occur, however, if a patient's serum contains antibodies from a previous exposure to the Lyme bacteria, even though the bacteria are gone. Such false positives could lead to unnecessary antibiotic treatments. Also, because the **antigenic** outer surface proteins of *Borrelia burgdorferi* are common to some other bacteria, they will react or cross-react with antibodies generated from other like-surfaced bacteria such as some gram-negative bacteria or other spirochetes.

WESTERN BLOTS

A Western blot is also an antigen/antibody-based test, but with greater specificity for *Borrelia burgdorferi* proteins. A sample of the patient's serum, along with samples of *Borrelia burgdorferi* proteins, is loaded into an electrophoresis gel. An electric charge runs through the gel, which separates the proteins by mass; the largest protein molecules remain near the top of the gel, while the smaller proteins are carried further down the gel. Figure 7.2 shows how an electrophoresis gel is used to detect *Borrelia burgdorferi* in birds.

After the proteins have been separated across the gel, the gel is covered with a special paper-like membrane and again subjected to an electric current. This transfers the proteins from the gel to the membrane. The membrane is washed with a solution containing fluorescent or radioactively tagged antibodies specific for *Borrelia burgdorferi*. The antibodies will attach to the *Borrelia burgdorferi* proteins on the membrane,

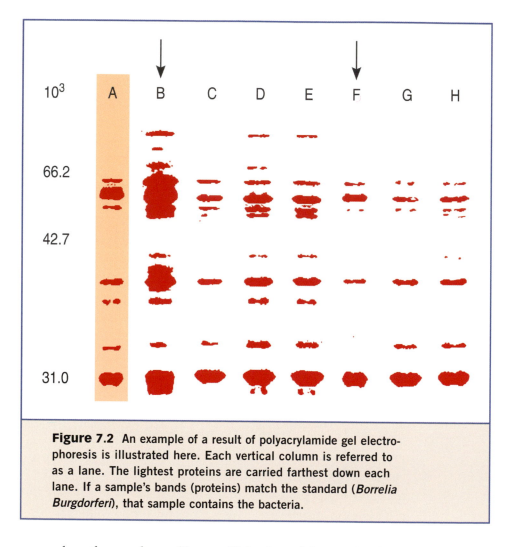

Figure 7.2 An example of a result of polyacrylamide gel electrophoresis is illustrated here. Each vertical column is referred to as a lane. The lightest proteins are carried farthest down each lane. If a sample's bands (proteins) match the standard (*Borrelia Burgdorferi*), that sample contains the bacteria.

where they can be readily seen. If the sizes of the proteins from the patient closely match those of *Borrelia burgdorferi*, the result is considered positive (Figure 7.3).

DNA PROBES

A polymerase chain reaction (PCR) test is particularly effective for diagnosing patients with later stages of infection. A sample of synovial fluid, which bathes the joints of the body, is taken from

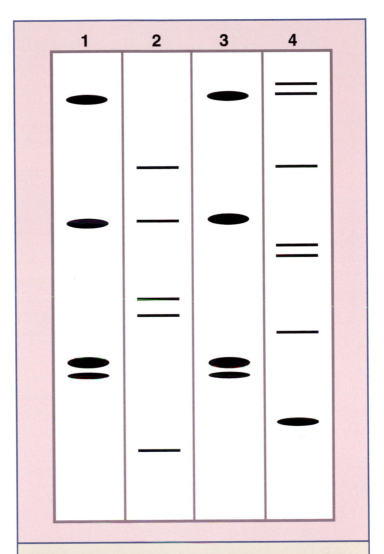

Figure 7.3 A Western blot is another diagnostic procedure based on antibody/antigen attachment. A sample is run on an electrophoresis gel, along with known *Borrelia Burgdorferi* proteins. The proteins separate according to mass, with the smallest proteins traveling the farthest down the gel. The gel is then placed on a special membrane and, via an electric current, the proteins are transferred to the membrane. The result is illustrated here.

the patient. DNA is extracted from the sample and is combined with a special enzyme that amplifies or multiplies the DNA. Then a specific DNA probe is used to detect the bacteria's DNA. In this case, the probe is a sequence of *Borrelia burgdorferi* genetic material. If this radioactive probe finds its complementary strand in the patient's DNA, the radioactive tag will attach to the strand, and the radioactivity can be detected. This would constitute a positive test result.

None of the Lyme disease diagnostic tests is foolproof. In addition to the technical problems mentioned above, laboratory error is a possibility. Any Lyme disease test results should be considered along with clinical data (i.e., symptoms such as swollen joints, stiff neck, red rash, fatigue) and epidemiological data (i.e., geography), before conclusions are drawn.

The importance of weighing tests, as well as clinical and epidemiological data, can best be seen when comparing Lyme disease with two other maladies that vex medical personnel—chronic fatigue syndrome and fibromyalgia. These three diseases share many symptoms (Figure 7.4) and medical personnel must gather as much data as possible before discerning between them.

EVOLUTIONARY ADAPTATIONS AND THE IMMUNE RESPONSE

It is important to treat Lyme disease with medications, as the body can not fight off the Lyme disease bacteria on its own. There is a reason why our bodies need help in fighting off the *Borrelia burgdorferi* bacteria and the resulting Lyme disease. This bacterium naturally wants to maximize its experience in the host (the body). Therefore, it has evolved two adaptations that allow it to continue living in us and to evade destruction by our immune system.

One of the first responses of the immune system to microbial invasion is the phagocytosis (or engulfment) of the invader

DIFFERENTIAL DIAGNOSIS OF PERSISTENT FATIGUE AND MYALGIA

Symptoms	Chronic Lyme disease	Chronic fatigue syndrome	Fibromyalgia
Fatigue/myalgias	+	+	+
Distal paresthesias	+	-	-
Localized radicular pain	+	-	-
Mental confusion	+	+	-
Memory deficits	+	+	-
Sore throat	-	+	-
Sleep disturbances	-	+	-
History of ECM or tick bite	+(80%)	-	-
Signs			
Crimson anterior pharyngeal pillars	-	+	-
Axillary adenopathy	-	+	-
Trigger-point tenderness	-	-	+
Arthritis/carditis	+	-	-
Meningitis/encephalopathy/neuritis	+	+/-	-

Figure 7.4 Lyme disease shares many symptoms with chronic fatigue syndrome and fibromyalgia, as can be seen on this chart. Fatigue is the most common symptom of all three diseases, while arthritis occurs only in patients afflicted with Lyme disease.

(Figure 7.5). A specialized white blood cell, known as a phagocyte (*phago* means "to eat" and *cyte* means "cell") encircles and engulfs the bacterium or infectious agent with two long pseudopodia or "arms." The white blood cell then destroys the bacterium.

One factor that appears to contribute to the virulence of *Borrelia burgdorferi* is that it can survive phagocytosis. *Borrelia burgdorferi* triggers a form of phagocytosis called coiling. Instead of engulfing the bacterium in one big "bite," the arms of the macrophage coil around the bacterium in many layers. **Lysosomes** (the cell's "garbage disposal") are prevented from degrading the bacterium completely. Although some pathogens are dissolved, the absence of strong hydrolytic enzymes allows some bacteria to survive and reproduce intracellularly within the macrophage itself. This induced coiling allows some bacteria to escape phagocytosis.

Borrelia burgdorferi invokes a different strategy to divert the other key response by the immune system—the humoral response. Normally, an invading antigen causes white blood cells called lymphocytes to mobilize in the body. These lymphocytes, which are specifically called B-lymphocytes, "read" the outer surface proteins of the bacteria and produce antibodies against the invading antigen. These antibodies then attach to those outer surface antigenic proteins, essentially flagging them so phagocytes can recognize and destroy the invader.

However, *Borrelia burgdorferi* has adapted to this defense mechanism. The outer membrane of *Borrelia burgdorferi* is coated with different lipoproteins called outer surface proteins. Antibodies are made by lymphocytes against these outer surface lipoproteins. *Borrelia burgdorferi* periodically changes its outer surface lipoproteins. Thus the antibodies do not recognize the bacterial cell and will not attack it. The humoral response of the body is compromised, and it lacks the ability to fight infection.

Phagocytosis

Phagocyte

Bacterium

Figure 7.5 Phagocytosis is one way that the body gets rid of foreign particles. A special type of white blood cell called a phagocyte stretches out "arms" and wraps them around the foreign particle, pulling it inside. Once the foreign particle (a bacterium in this diagram) is inside the white blood cell, special enzymes begin to degrade the bacterium.

TREATMENT

Lyme disease treatment is no different than that for any other disease having a spirochete etiological agent: the earlier the treatment, the better the results. The dosage and duration of treatment depend on the assessment of disease severity by medical professionals. For adults, nonpregnant women, and older children, one of the following antibiotics may be given in the following doses:

- Tetracycline, 250–500 mg four times daily for 10 to 21 days.

- Doxycycline, 50–100 mg twice daily for 10 to 21 days.

- * Phenoxymethyl penicillin, 250–500 mg four times daily for 10 to 21 days.

- Amoxicillin, 250–500 mg four times daily for 10 to 21 days.

- Azithromycin, one 250 mg capsule twice daily for two weeks.

* Also for pregnant women, lactating women, and children.

Adults who are allergic to one of the recommended antibiotics may take 250–500 mg of erythromycin four times daily for 10 to 21 days. Data have shown this antibiotic to be slightly less effective than tetracycline, doxycycline, phenoxymethyl penicillin, and amoxicillin. Children who are allergic to the other antibiotics may also take erythromycin, but the appropriate dosage must be determined by a medical professional.

For patients in the later stages of the disease, hospitalization and intravenous antibiotic therapy is usually the treatment of choice. Antibiotics seek out and destroy the bacteria, some by rupturing the organism's cell envelope.

The problem with late-stage Lyme disease is that the bacteria have had time to drill deep into tissues and have become hard to reach with antibiotics. Also, there is more variability in the treatment of late-stage Lyme disease because of different individual rates of disease progression and different patient responses to treatments. Some patients develop a treatment-resistant chronic condition, while others see their symptoms disappear months or years after oral or

NAPPING WITH DARWIN

Many people are familiar with Charles Darwin's famous voyage on the H.M.S. *Beagle* (1831–1836). For almost five years, Darwin traveled around the world, collecting data that eventually aided in the formulation of his theory of evolution. Many people do not realize, however, that this voyage was his first and last significant natural history excursion.

Darwin, often called the Father of Modern Biology, was renowned for his grasp of natural selection. With a first-hand knowledge of the diversity of life and the selection pressures that come to bear on it, he could predict the presence of organisms not yet discovered. Yet, unknown to him, the very natural selection engine he knew so well was at work inside his body.

Darwin was often fatigued and needed frequent naps. This was inconvenient, as it interrupted his work. What he did not know, but can be inferred from studies of his journals and photographic portraits, is that he was infected with the **pathogenic** microbe that causes sleeping sickness. Researchers believe that Darwin was bitten by a tritomid bug, which is the vector for the infectious agent, *Trypanosoma cruzi*, a single-celled protist. This microbe has evolved the same capability as the bacterium *Borrelia burgdorferi* to avoid detection by the immune system. Science historians feel Darwin was infected while in South America. He would suffer from this disease for 40 years. He died in 1882.

intravenous treatment (treatment administered directly through a vein). Treatment depends on clinical analysis of the course of the disease. Dosage and amounts should be determined by a medical professional.

For patients with neurological symptoms such as meningitis or brain and spinal fluid involvement, cephalosporins (bacteriocidal medications that are capable of penetrating nervous tissue) are used. Suggested bacteriocidal agents include:

- Ceftriaxone (Rocephin®) given intravenously.

- Cefotaxime (Claforan®) given intravenously.

- Cefuroxime (Ceftin®) given orally.

For patients with cardiac problems (e.g., **atrioventricular block**, acute **myopericarditis**), the treatment regimen depends on the degree of involvement of the disease with the tissue. If the tissue results in mild atrioventricular block, tetracycline is effective. Those with myopericarditis should receive an anti-inflammatory drug in addition to antibiotic therapy. Patients with more severe cardiac involvement should be treated with ceftriaxone as above.

People with arthritic conditions have used oral regimens of doxycycline and amoxicillin, usually on higher doses to assure effectiveness. Children have used phenoxymethyl penicillin for this condition. Penicillin G has also been used in both adults and children with Lyme arthritis, although some sources report minimal effectiveness.

In addition to standard antibiotic therapy, other treatments are being used, some of which are being touted on the Internet. For example, the hyperbaric chamber raises the oxygen level of the body and has been used successfully to treat gangrene. However, gangrene is caused by *Clostridium* bacterium, an anaerobe, whose metabolism functions in the absence of oxygen and, in this case, is poisoned by oxygen. Thus, increasing the amount of oxygen in the body will kill this type of bacteria. *Borrelia burgdorferi*, on the other hand, is an aerobic bacterium and, as such, needs oxygen to survive. There is some evidence of beneficial treatments when the hyperbaric chamber is used with Lyme patients in combination with antibiotic therapy. Advocates of this treatment claim the increased oxygen under pressure helps the antibiotic reach the bacteria. More data are needed, however, to support this treatment for Lyme disease.

8

The Lyme Vaccine

One of the greatest public health victories of the last century was the discovery of safe and effective vaccines.

—Gro Harlem Brundtland, Director-General, World Health Organization

As the emerging threat of Lyme disease became known, the clamor for a vaccine grew louder. After all, not only have millions of lives been saved with vaccines, but also many millions have been relieved of the very threat of such diseases as polio and smallpox, following the development of effective vaccines. In the 1990s, when biotechnology demonstrated that such widely used vaccinations as the diphtheria-pertussis-typhoid (DPT) shot could be made even safer using recombinant DNA technology (the new vaccine is known as DPaT), it was widely accepted that a vaccine could be used to eradicate Lyme disease.

Before 1998, there were only two approaches to Lyme disease. One was to take a preventive approach. This involved having an awareness of Lyme disease **risk factors**, such as geographical location and the habitat where ticks are common. The other tactic was to be aware and reactive. If a person found that a black-legged tick had attached to the skin, he or she could take an antibiotic. Of course, it is also possible to combine the two approaches.

Although both approaches have their merits, each also has limitations. A preventive approach requires an educational campaign. Such campaigns, although energetically launched by the Lyme Borreliosis Foundation in 1988 and the American Arthritis Foundation and other groups, involved considerable resources. Results were uneven and, to a certain extent, depended on the receptivity of the region or locality.

Those concerned with the complex problem of resistance to antibiotics quickly challenged the reactive approach. It was felt that some people,

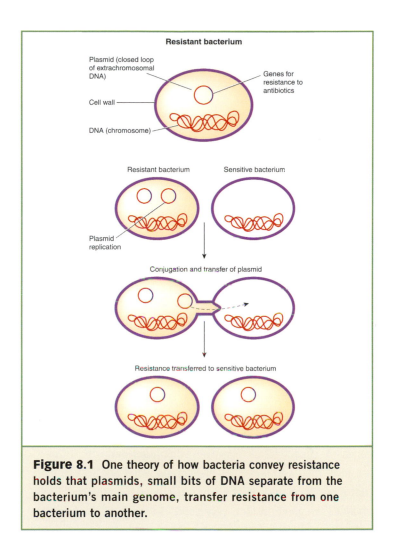

Figure 8.1 One theory of how bacteria convey resistance holds that plasmids, small bits of DNA separate from the bacterium's main genome, transfer resistance from one bacterium to another.

especially those quite aware of the debilitating effects of chronic Lyme disease, were overusing antibiotics. For example, people who had been bitten by any tick, including non-black-legged ticks, would demand an antibiotic from medical professionals, contributing to the increasing problem of antibiotic resistance in certain bacteria (Figure 8.1).

Therefore, when the advisory panel to the Food and Drug Administration (FDA) recommended a vaccine, many were relieved, particularly in **endemic** areas. In May 1998, the vaccine, called LYMErix® and produced by GlaxoSmithKline, was approved for sale. Many thought this was the ultimate answer.

VACCINE BASICS AND THE IMMUNE RESPONSE

To better understand how the Lyme disease vaccine works, it is necessary to discuss some important biotechnological techniques. Acquired immunity can occur in various ways. It can happen naturally without medical intervention—e.g., a baby acquires its mother's antibodies for a short period after birth. It can also be acquired artificially with medical assistance—e.g., through a vaccine. It can happen without active engagement

ANTIBIOTIC RESISTANCE

Charles Darwin thought that evolution was too slow to be observed. When he collected the fossils of sea animals high in the Chilean Andes of South America, he correctly inferred that it took millennia for the fossils to arrive there. He could not know that modern medicine would speed things up and set the stage for observable evolution.

Mutations are the stuff of evolution. These changes in the genes are usually lethal. However, when considering that there are more than a trillion types of bacteria, what are the chances that a mutation adds to the survivability of the species? The chances are good, in fact, very good. So when we continually bathe bacteria with a chemical, such as an antibiotic, to kill them, we are really on a search-and-destroy mission. We usually kill just about all of them. This is a problem, however. The few that survive are not harmed by the antibiotic and are considered antibiotic resistant. These resistant bacteria reproduce and grow in great numbers, easily out-competing those bacteria that are susceptible to antibiotics. They are also now genetically resistant to that antibiotic of choice. The result is that bacterial infections that were once easily treated with specific antibiotics, may become resistant to treatment by those same antibiotics.

of the immune system (passive), or involve lymphocytes and antibody production (active). These immunities can occur in four possible combinations:

- *Naturally acquired passive immunity* occurs when a soon-to-be mother passes the immune substance IgG across the placenta to the developing fetus.

- *Naturally acquired active immunity* occurs when an individual is exposed to disease. This initiates the immune response, including antibody production.

- *Artificially acquired passive immunity* can be initiated by taking antibodies from a person or another animal and injecting them into the patient. Activation of the immune system is not involved.

- *Artificially acquired active immunity* occurs through a vaccine. The immune system is stimulated to produce antibodies. It is this last category of immunity that is involved in the Lyme disease vaccine.

Artificially acquired active immunity is usually induced by injecting the individual with an attenuated (weakened) form of the pathogenic organism to create immunity to that organism. The pathogen has been mostly deactivated by heat or other means. Some attenuated organisms are created by growing them at warmer or cooler temperatures than their natural habitat, which weakens the organisms. When injected into a human host, they do not grow as well, and the patient's immune system has time to develop antibodies before the organisms can cause disease. Although vaccines made from attenuated organisms are safe, occasionally some patients experience more of the target disease's symptoms than would be considered healthy.

To avoid the small risk of symptoms associated with attenuated vaccines, scientists have used recombinant DNA technology to generate just the antigen-displaying portion of the organism. This allows the body to form antibodies, but the organism does not have the capability to cause disease. LYMErix®, the first vaccine for Lyme disease, is an example of this newer type of vaccine.

LYMERIX

The Lyme disease vaccine, LYMErix®, was developed using this recombinant DNA technology. Because outer surface protein A (OspA) dominates the outer surface of *Borrelia burgdorferi*, it was the antigenic surface used in the vaccine. The gene responsible for expressing OspA, located on a linear plasmid of *Borrelia burgdorferi*, was first removed from the plasmid and copied using polymerase chain reaction technology, or PCR. These genes were then placed in nonpathogenic *E. coli* cells, where they expressed themselves to produce outer surface proteins exactly like *Borrelia burgdorferi*. These proteins constitute the vaccine, which is injected into individuals. As these outer surface proteins are antigenic, antibodies are then made against them, conferring protection against Lyme disease.

During the approval process, GlaxoSmithKline, the maker of LYMErix®, showed through a study of 10,936 people in endemic states that the vaccine was 79% effective at preventing Lyme disease after the full regime was implemented. The company began producing and distributing LYMErix® after receiving approval to do so by the Food and Drug Administration (FDA) in January 1999. Because antibody titers (amounts) tend to drop quickly, the recommended regimen was a booster shot one month after the initial vaccination, and a third dose a year later. The Advisory Committee on Immunization Practices of the Centers for Disease Control and Prevention (CDC) suggested that people in the age range of 15 to 70 years who live, work, or play in areas of high risk should consider getting the vaccination. They also stated that patients who were treated for early Lyme disease were also candidates for the vaccine, as their antibody titers would not be sufficient to fight off the bacteria. The CDC also clearly stated that children, those with chronic Lyme arthritis, and people with minimal exposure to ticks, should not receive the vaccine.

THE CONTROVERSY

In November 2002, GlaxoSmithKline announced that they removed LYMErix®, the only available Lyme disease vaccine, from the market. The company claimed that their projections showed too few cases of Lyme disease in the near future to justify the cost of producing the vaccine. But there is more to the LYMErix® story.

Soon after the FDA approved LYMErix® in 1999, complaints about side effects, mostly arthritis-like symptoms, began to emerge. These culminated in a FDA hearing based on these complaints in February 2002. The FDA had received 1,048 reports from those complaining of various side effects from the vaccine. There were other accusations that doctors did not explain the potential for side effects of the vaccine, nor did they divulge that some patients in GlaxoSmithKline's trial studies had voiced concerns about the way the trials were conducted. For example, one patient claimed that researchers refused to record her symptoms. A common complaint was the onset of arthritis after receiving the vaccination. (One theory as to why this occurs is that the vaccine initiates an autoimmune response in which the body attacks its own tissues, especially in people who carry the **HLA-4 gene**.)

One GlaxoSmithKline safety study during the approval process appears to refute any correlation betweeen the vaccine and arthritis. LYMErix® was given to 5,000 people while another 5,000 people were given placebos. Arthritis symptoms developed in only two percent of the people, regardless of whether they received the real vaccine or the placebos. As the presence of the HLA-4 gene was random throughout both study groups, the conclusion was that the vaccine did not precipitate an autoimmune response in the body.

The FDA expressed frustration with GlaxoSmithKline, which had promised a study of much higher power (involving 25,000 subjects) after approval. As of February 2002, only 3,600 people were enrolled in the study. The vaccine was removed from the shelves in fall 2002. With the only vaccine pulled from the market and none others waiting for approval, the burden of Lyme disease prevention falls to personal and community actions.

9

Prevention

I do not direct my speech only to those who are already affected with sickness, but to them rather which yet injoy their good and perfect health, to the end they may serve themselves with measures proper to maintaine the same. For how pretious and deare a treasure it is to be of good health.

—John Ghesel, *The Rule of Health*, 1631

Lyme disease is not contagious; that is, it is not communicable from person to person. Therefore, prevention of the infection involves an awareness of the tick's habitat, the animals involved in this zoonosis, and what to do when a black-legged tick attaches to the skin. This awareness can greatly reduce both an individual's risk and fear of the disease.

RISK FACTORS

Preventing Lyme disease is based on knowing the risk factors involved in acquiring the disease and limiting or eliminating them. For example, knowledge of geography is primary in the prevention of Lyme disease. If one were visiting relatives or vacationing out of state, it would be worthwhile to consider the entire geography of the United States and Lyme risk factors within each region. A national Lyme disease risk map is produced by the Centers for Disease Control and Prevention's Division of Vector-Borne Infectious Diseases based on information from field research (Figure 9.1).

The map in Figure 9.1 shows two high-risk areas for Lyme disease. The areas of highest risk—the darkest areas—are along the New England coast, including a number of areas that stretch considerably inland, and the border areas, with exception, between Minnesota and Wisconsin. The other noticeable area is the large patch of minimal or no risk—the lightest areas—

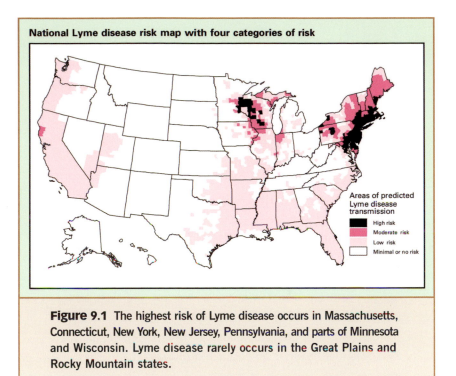

National Lyme disease risk map with four categories of risk

Areas of predicted
Lyme disease
transmission

■ High risk
■ Moderate risk
□ Low risk
□ Minimal or no risk

Figure 9.1 The highest risk of Lyme disease occurs in Massachusetts, Connecticut, New York, New Jersey, Pennsylvania, and parts of Minnesota and Wisconsin. Lyme disease rarely occurs in the Great Plains and Rocky Mountain states.

stretching from the Rocky Mountains to the Great Plains, down to the southwestern states.

When planning to travel to another state, it is important to refer to that state's health department and epidemiology division for a state-wide Lyme disease risk map, or something approximating it (i.e., map of confirmed Lyme disease cases). In Connecticut, for example, the highest risk for Lyme disease would be in the southeastern coastal area of the state. As this area is popular for seashore vacations, one would have to be particularly careful if venturing off sandy beaches and established pathways to edge habitat where ticks abound. These particulars, of course, will vary from state to state. For instance, determine whether there are large blocks of continuous forest where you live or are visiting or whether they are fragmented. A person would have a considerably higher risk of encountering the tick vector in the latter environment than in the former,

RISK FACTORS AND
LIVING THE GOOD LIFE

In the early 1930s, Helen and Scott Nearing left New York City to live in Pikes Falls, Vermont, for what they hoped would be "the good life." They asked themselves if they had improved their chances for good health by such a move. By studying statistical data and their early experiences in Vermont, they found they had actually not improved their chances. People in Vermont had similar health problems as people who lived in New York City. The Nearings sought out a definition of what it meant to be healthy.

The Nearings looked in medical journals and searched medical libraries. They found considerable material on disease but very little on what it meant to be healthy and even less on how to pursue a healthy life. They approached many medical professionals with the same question. In one instance they were told that health is an absence of disease. Later, they were told that disease is an absence of health. Recognizing this circular argument, they set about developing a lifestyle that led to mental, physical, and social well-being by reducing risk factors.

The Nearings raised their own food, free of chemical pesticides and chemical fertilizers. They blended physical work on their homestead with writing and music. They actively participated in the issues and events of their time. The Nearings viewed these activities as integral to a healthy, balanced lifestyle. Scott Nearing died at 100 years of age of his own free will. He simply stopped eating. Helen Nearing died in a car accident when she was 95 years old. Their book, *Living The Good Life, How to Live Sanely and Simply in a Troubled World*, has become a very popular text on how to reduce one's risk factors and enhance one's health.

due to more edge habitat and the dilution effect (see "Lyme Disease, Biodiversity, and the Dilution Effect," page 50).

DEER TICK INDEX

Some areas of the country have created unique ways of assessing risk and getting important Lyme disease risk data to people. A collaboration of the Louis Calder Center, which is a biological field station at Fordham University, and the American Lyme Disease Foundation have developed just such a unique tool. Dr. Thomas Daniels and Dr. Richard Falco of the field station's Vector Ecology Laboratory of Westchester County, New York, have initiated a Deer Tick Index. Data is collected on tick abundance on a weekly basis. This information is combined with historical data of tick activity that have been collected since 1987.

Risk of a nymph or adult deer tick attaching itself to a person is then rated on a 10-point scale according to tick abundance and historical data:

- 1 = Low risk. Enjoy the outdoors, but still take precautions.

- 5 = Moderate risk. Be alert, and take precautions.

- 10 = High risk. Limit exposure, and use extreme caution. Consider going to indoor activities.

The index is calculated by midweek for the coming weekend. The American Lyme Disease Foundation then gives this information to the media and health professionals. The index is considered valid for suburban areas of New York, New Jersey, and Connecticut.

EDGE HABITAT AND RISK OF EXPOSURE

Next to general geographic and historical knowledge, the most immediate concern is the type of habitat to be encountered. These habitat characteristics determine the variety of species that can be sustained and are referred to as beta-diversity. Many ticks are found in the transitional zones called edge habitat. Although some edge habitat occurs naturally—depending on soil and wind—this kind of transitional vegetation zone is often man-made. It quite often represents a grass-to-shrubs and tree seedlings-to-forest transition. A lawn abutting woodland or a roadway cutting through a forest are just two examples of man-made edge habitat. In New England, for example, an abandoned farm field, marked by a rock wall, will surround a meadow that is kept as such by grazing wildlife and generates ample edge habitat. It is important to remember that avoiding outdoor activities may not be enough. Cats or dogs explore edge habitat frequently and may bring infected ticks home.

When planning outdoor activities, it is important to consider the immediate habitat and the time of year to calculate the level of Lyme disease risk. In New England, for example, risk is much higher in summer months when ticks are questing for a blood meal. The host mammals and birds, as well as people, are much more active during this season. However, it is important to be careful during other seasons too. If other risk factors are present (i.e., geography, history, edge habitat, host species), then tick attachment and Lyme disease can occur. Tick index readings as high as 8 have been issued in late November at the Vector Ecology Laboratory in New York.

PROTECTION DURING OUTDOOR ACTIVITIES

A number of preventive steps should be taken before engaging in outdoor activities where a number of risk factors are present.

- Wear light colored clothing, so ticks can easily be seen and removed.

- Wear long sleeves and a hat.

- Tuck pant legs into socks. Always wear closed footwear.

- Tuck shirt into pants.

Most of these steps prevent the tick's access to skin. It is important not to take these steps lightly. One study by the United States Armed Forces found that the incidence of tick attachments can be cut in half by simply tucking pants into boots.

While outdoors, avoid brushing through edge habitat. Because ticks can neither fly nor jump, they will position themselves at the end of vegetation in order to attach to a host. If hiking, try to stay in the middle of the trail. Avoid sitting directly on vegetation where possible. If picnicking, sit in established areas (benches and/or rocks) and not on the grass. During the activity, check both yourself and your pets for ticks.

After a being outside, brush off clothing thoroughly. Wash clothing and shower within a short time. Check body folds, especially lower extremities and armpits for ticks. Ticks quite often search over body surfaces for several hours before attaching, so the above steps can be effective preventive measures. Remember, it is possible to brush off a tick, especially in the larval or nymph stage, without ever having seen it.

REPELLENTS

There are two chemicals, DEET (N,N-diethyl-m-tolumide) and Permethrin, marketed as effective repellents against ticks. Each has their advantages and disadvantages. DEET is the most widely used tick repellent, partly because it is also an insect repellent. It is suggested to use it in concentrations not to exceed 33% DEET. Although container directions instruct to apply it to the skin, there are DEET devotees who apply it to clothing only.

One of the problems with DEET is that 20% of a skin application gets absorbed into the blood stream. Certainly, even a careful clothing application may result in some DEET touching the skin surface. Long-term consequences of such exposures are not known. It is toxic if ingested. The Connecticut Department of Health has developed precautions concerning DEET:

- Avoid prolonged and excessive use.

- Use products with 20% to 30% DEET.

- Use sparingly, no more than one or two times a day.

- Avoid inhaling or ingesting DEET.

- Keep repellent out of eyes.

- Avoid use on damaged skin such as sunburn or cuts.

Container directions indicate to apply the repellent to the outside of clothing, never the inside. Pregnant and nursing women are especially directed not to apply DEET to their skin. Children should never apply it to their hands or near their mouths or eyes. See manufacturer's guidelines as to which clothing is adversely affected by DEET. It is advisable to wash all clothes and shower immediately after an outdoor activity in which DEET has been used.

Permethrin is a neurotoxin that is effective against ticks and insects. It is recommended that it be applied to clothing and not skin surfaces. It can be found as an aerosol spray, rinse, and cream. The latter two require a physician's prescription because they are used to treat scabies, a skin disease caused by mites. The skin application is rinsed off in a set period of time. The spray is said to last up to six weeks on clothing, even if washed with detergent, and still be effective. Permethrin is not as readily absorbed by the skin as DEET. Permethrin should not be confused with pyrethrins, which is the natural insecticide found in chrysanthemums. Although permethrin has chemical similarities to the natural insecticide, it is synthetically produced.

Data show that most black-legged ticks are found 1–2 yards from woodland edges. Often, in New England, this environment is a rock wall with a woodland backdrop. With this information in mind, some homeowners spray permethrin on cotton balls and place these in used paper towel or toilet paper cardboard cylinders along these woodland boundaries. Mice then use the cotton for nests and ticks are killed in the process.

The chemical is purported not to harm mice. Easy access to other hosts, such as voles, gray squirrels, eastern chipmunks, and birds, especially ground-dwelling birds (e.g., robins, mourning doves), may reduce the impact of this approach.

A similar product, a tick bait box, uses a chemical called fipronil. In 1999, the CDC tested a ten-acre area with 125 fipronil tick bait boxes. Scientists found 80% fewer ticks in the treated area than in an untreated area.

Although these repellents have been found to be effective, their use is controversial. Permethrin, for example, is a suspected carcinogen. There are individuals who elect to take the preventive steps presented here without using chemicals.

TICK REMOVAL

It is not necessary to use extreme measures, such as burning or smothering, to remove a tick. Not only are these methods ineffective, they may well agitate the tick to release the bacteria and infect the host. One man contracted Rocky Mountain spotted fever when he removed a tick from his dog and smashed the tick with a hammer. He was infected when the dog's blood contained in the tick splashed into his eye. Ticks, like sharks and wolves, have been stigmatized by many, especially in myths, as purveyors of evil. They, like other animals, are organisms filling a particular niche or lifestyle. Their adaptations equip them to carry out two activities: attach to animals and suck their blood. Intentions of a conscious kind, on the dark side or otherwise, are not involved.

The following steps should be used to remove a tick (Figure 9.2):

1. Using a pair of tweezers, clasp the tick as close to the place of attachment to your skin as possible. Tweezers that have a flat end are best as they allow you to get parallel to your skin.

2. With one firm continuous upward motion, remove the tick.

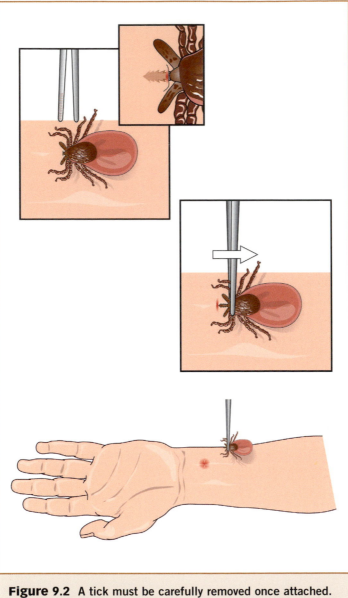

Figure 9.2 A tick must be carefully removed once attached. Special care must be taken not to burst the tick, as its blood may be infected with Lyme bacteria. Grab the tick with a pair of flat-head tweezers, as close to the skin as possible. Then, pull upward firmly to remove the tick. Wash the area with antiseptic.

3. Save the tick in a small plastic bottle if identification is a question. Label the bottle with name, address, date, and an estimate of how long the tick was attached to you.

4. An antiseptic can be used at the former site of attachment.

5. Wash hands with soap and water and disinfect the tweezers in boiling water or with alcohol.

Current data show that it usually takes a minimum attachment of 24 hours before the Lyme bacteria are transmitted to a human host. Therefore, removing a tick in a timely manner is imperative.

PREVENTING INFECTION IN PETS

Dogs, cats, horses, and other domestic animals can be infected with the Lyme bacteria. The symptoms in dogs, which are similar for other animals, are as follows:

- Lameness, e.g., back legs collapse

- Sudden severe pain

- Loss of appetite

- Fever

- Depression

- Arthritis

Taken individually, these symptoms, particularly lameness and loss of appetite, can be indicative of several maladies, including Lyme disease. A veterinarian should be consulted, since both Lyme disease and other diseases are possible.

Dogs and cats are particularly susceptible to tick attachment as they are close to ground level and, in this sense, continually sampling the environment. This is particularly true for long-haired pets. For example, animal researchers feel dogs have

6 to 10 times greater exposure to Lyme disease than humans. Checking animals for ticks after they have been outdoors and removing any attached ticks is important. An effective vaccine was available for animals, including dogs, before one was available for humans. They are still available with booster vaccinations suggested on a yearly basis.

LONG-TERM SOLUTIONS
Pesticides

Some people consider widespread application of pesticides to the environment as part of the longer-term solutions to Lyme disease. Those pesticides that kill ticks are called **acaricides**. They may also function as insecticides. Examples are carbaryl, known by the brand name Sevin®, and chlorpyrifos, known by the brand name Dursban®.

There are numerous problems with pesticides. Spraying edge and wooded areas quite often does not reach the ticks, either on vegetation or on animal hosts, because it settles on higher vegetation and ticks like to live closer to the ground. These chemicals are also known to adversely affect other animals. Even more daunting are the possible effects on humans, especially if these agents are mishandled.

Both of these chemicals are petroleum based. They function as toxins to neuromuscular junctions by inhibiting cholinesterase—an enzyme that normally breaks down acetylcholine, which is released by nerve endings to stimulate muscle. Without the cholinesterase, continual stimulation results in tremors and the eventual death of the organism. This chemical is similar to chemicals developed for chemical warfare.

Humans unduly exposed to these chemicals, which can be absorbed through the skin, have experienced excessive salivation and twitching of muscles. There is limited data on long-term deficiency in mental performance in patients who were overexposed to this chemical. There is further environmental concern as some of these pesticides have been detected in ground water. Data are not sufficient to us to draw conclusions about long-term effects. Unease concerning these issues has led to the search for a non-chemical long-term solution.

DESIGNER TICKS?

The common response to vector-borne diseases has been to eradicate the vector. For example, the insecticide DDT was used to kill mosquitoes, which carry the malarian parasite. The introduction of this synthetic toxin into the environment, however, has brought mixed results. It had unforeseen harmful effects on wildlife, such as bringing the osprey, a fish-eating coastal bird, to the brink of extinction. The chemical even surfaced in human breast milk. Mosquitoes eventually developed a resistance to DDT. Consequently, both the use and production of DDT have been banned in the United States.

Some geneticists suggest that biotechnology can help prevent the spread of malaria. To do this, they have produced genetically modified mosquitoes. A scientist would insert foreign DNA into fertilized mosquito eggs using a very tiny needle. This DNA would enable mosquito offspring to produce an enzyme that would kill the malarian parasite. Mating with mosquitoes in the wild would then (ideally) spread this genetic capability.

Because *Borrelia burgdorferi* resides in salivary glands, genetically altering ticks may seem to be a solution to preventing Lyme disease. *Borrelia burgdorferi* is also present in tick intestines, so killing the microbe in one area alone probably would not be sufficient. Also, some of the same objections being raised against other designer insects apply to ticks. Once the genetically altered ticks are released into the environment, the aftereffects, particularly negative ones, are uncertain. For example, the designer tick may become a carrier of another disease. Many questions about the advantages and disadvantages of genetically modified species remain.

Biological Control

One way to avoid chemical pesticides is to seek out an already existing biological control such as natural predator or parasite. For example, this was done in an attempt to control the gypsy moth infestation of the 1970s and 1980s in North America. Gypsy moths were denuding East Coast trees of their leaves. It was found that the bacteria, *Bacillus thurlinginsis* (Bt), produced toxins that disrupted the pupal stage of moth development. With regard to ticks, however, we have little experience with the use of biological controls.

The black-legged tick is parasitized by a tiny wasp, *Hunterellus hookeri* (the wasp lives inside the tick). One record of an attempt to control ticks with this wasp was on Naushon Island, Massachusetts, in 1926. Here the target was the American dog tick, *Dermacentor variabilis*, which is often confused with the black-legged tick. No wasps were found in *Dermacentor variabilis*, and there was no appreciable reduction in dog ticks here or in other places where this was attempted. Furthermore, the wasp seems to be unable to establish itself anywhere in substantial numbers, and this parasite is scarce where black-legged ticks abound. The general conclusion thus far is that the wasp would not be an effective biological control.

Reducing the Number of Deer

Invariably, long-term solutions focus on white-tailed deer because they are the almost exclusive preferred hosts for the adult ticks. White-tailed deer have added importance, as they are involved in the reproductive stage of the tick life cycle. Deer abundance correlates with both the emergence of Lyme disease as well as its persistence. Acaricides, chemicals toxic to ticks, have been used experimentally on deer to control tick populations. This was attempted on Great Island, in West Yarmouth, Massachusetts, in the 1980s. Ninety-nine volunteers were involved in trapping and placing the acaricides on the deer. Six recaptured deer were found to have as many ticks on them as first-time captures. Thus, this approach was deemed unsuccessful.

Another partial solution would be to initiate infertility in a population of deer. This has been done using tranquilizing darts on female deer (does) and injecting immunocontraceptives once the deer are sedated. This prevents the deer from conceiving offspring. Another similar method leads to abortions. Both methods, unfortunately, have to be performed annually to be effective, and thus they become quite expensive. The Connecticut Agricultural Station is presently researching a method of male deer sterilization.

Removal of deer, primarily by hunting, has also been studied. This research was also conducted on Great Island. Half the deer herd was removed by hunting. The abundance of larval ticks was not affected the following year. When the rest of the herd was removed, except for two survivors, the various life-stages of ticks eventually diminished. An interesting aside to this study was that with removal of deer on Great Island, there was simultaneously an increase in ticks on nearby Nantucket Island, where the deer population was free to roam and reproduce.

Removal of deer by hunting has come under increasing debate. Many hunters want the antlers of the male deer for trophy purposes and thus will only hunt the males, leaving many does to reproduce. The *New York Times*, in a lead editorial on December 2, 2002, called for the increased hunting of does as a partial solution to Lyme disease and deer-related traffic accidents. More than 1 million deer are struck by vehicles each year, and more than 100 people die as a result. Some states have initiated incentives for hunters to kill does. This has brought outcries from animal rights activists and others. Also, unless removal is performed in a very restricted geographic area (e.g., islands), it appears to be only a temporary remedy. The deer simply repopulate the area.

Ecologists have long noted that when animals, especially herd animals, reach exceptionally high numbers that are unsustainable in terms of the amount of space, natural selection occurs, usually in the form of disease. This seems to be occurring in the United States. A chronic wasting disease that affects the brain of deer and elk is on the rise. It seems to have the spongy brain characteristic of "mad cow disease." Unlike mad cow disease, it does not seem transferable to people who eat the deer or elk meat, although studies are in early stages. As of 2002, chronic wasting disease occurred in five states and seems to be making its way eastward. Hunters, especially those in states with large deer populations, are voicing the most concern over this disease. What impact this malady will have on Lyme disease is not clear.

Long-term solutions to huge deer populations are very much needed. Reintroduction of extirpated predators (such as wolves) will have some limited utility in regions with large forest expanses such as Maine and New York State. These reintroductions would have to be accompanied by substantial educational campaigns by state and environmental groups to combat the many myths about wolves and to get feedback from the people living there. Such measures are an important way to address both real and imagined fears. Even if these reintroductions were successful, many questions remain such as would the number of ticks per adult deer increase with herd reduction?

Data on forest fragmentation are considerable, especially concerning its long-term impact on fauna. However, few data exist on how this affects vectors and disease risk. Felicia Keesing, a biologist at Bard College, conducted an experiment on the human impacts on landscape and on Lyme disease risk. She focused on tick density in 14 forest patches in Dutchess County, New York. She found that the density of infected ticks was higher in forest blocks of less than five acres versus larger forested areas.

One way to begin mitigating this fragmentation trend is natural long-term habitat alteration. This could be accomplished by allowing certain state and federal forests to mature to old growth. This would reduce habitat fragmentation and the edge habitat favored by deer; thus, in part, denying adult black-legged ticks their favorite host. To be most effective, this approach would have to be in combination with sustainable developmental patterns for both town and country that take disease risk into consideration.

CONCLUSION

Lyme disease was one of the new, emerging diseases of the last quarter of the twentieth century. It quickly became our number one vector-borne disease and helped topple what some overly optimistic scientists of the late 1960s claimed was the end of infectious disease. In many ways, it is a classic vector-borne disease with animal hosts harboring the bacteria, acting as vectors and transmitting the disease to humans. It differs from other well-known vector-borne diseases, such as sleeping sickness and malaria, in that its symptoms can mimic those of other diseases.

Lyme disease history shows the strength of interdisciplinary sciences, such as medical epidemiology and ecology, in determining its cause or **etiology**. Lyme disease also gives us the chance to see evolution happening in front of our very eyes with mutation of the Lyme bacteria, *Borrelia* species, and antibiotic resistance, that evolutionary tug of war between the immune system and microbes.

At the same time, Lyme disease shows the promise and pitfalls of the newest interdisciplinary science—biotechnology. Was a bioengineered vaccine rushed to market before it was fully field tested? It has been pulled from the shelves for conflicting reasons. Will there be a safe biotechnical answer to Lyme disease so that both personal and collective recourse to chemical repellants and pesticides can be avoided? Will diseases be considered when towns vote on plans of development and conservation? Hopefully these pages have provided both the data and the approaches necessary to grapple with these questions as the new millennium unfolds.

Glossary

Acaricide—A pesticide that specifically kills ticks.

Antigenic—Capable of causing the production of antibodies.

Antiglobulin—An antibody that sticks to a protein, which can be another antibody.

Arachnid—The family of arthropods that have eight legs, no antennae, and heads and thoraxes that are fused together.

Arthropod—An animal having jointed appendages and a segmented body. Insects and arachnids, including mites and ticks, are included in this group.

Atrioventricular Block—A block that prevents proper blood flow between heart chambers.

Biogeography—Study of the distribution of fauna and flora.

Clinical—Work based on actual observation and treatment of patients.

Compromised—Lacking resistence to disease.

Dementia—A decline in mental function including memory loss and impairment of task execution.

Ecological Imbalance—The displacement of an organism from an environment that results in an overabundance of another organism.

Ecological Introduction—An organism that enters an area where it is not normally found.

Emerging—New; coming into existence.

Endemic—A persistent presence in a certain geographic population.

Epidemiologist—A scientist who studies disease patterns.

Epidemiology—The study of the prevalence and patterns of diseases.

Etiology—The study of the causes of disease.

Fauna—Animals.

Fitness—The ability of an organism to reproduce and pass on its traits to the next generation.

Flora—Plants.

Genome—The main DNA molecule(s) of an organism.

HLA-4 Gene—Human leukocyte antigen gene in which the body's plasma cells have difficulty recognizing their own cells.

Host—An organism which nourishes a parasite.

Humoral—The response of the body's immune system that produces antibodies.

Infectious—Caused by a pathogenic microorganism or agent.

Lysosome—A saclike cellular organelle that contains various hydrolytic enzymes.

Myopericarditis—An inflammation of the muscle and membranes of the heart.

Neurotoxin—A poison that affects the nervous system.

Omnivores—Animals that eat both plants and other animals.

Pathogenesis—The development of a disease.

Pathogenic—Disease causing.

Plasmids—Small circular DNA molecules found only in bacteria. A single bacterium may have many of these.

Polymerase Chain Reaction—The process by which a segment of DNA can be copied and reproduced.

Preferred Habitat—The area selected by an animal to carry out its life history.

Protist—Single-celled organisms that have organelles (i.e., nuclei, mitochondria), unlike bacteria which have no organelles.

Reservoir—A host harboring a parasite and allowing it to carry out significant aspects of its life cycle.

Risk Factors—Elements that predispose an individual to disease.

Strains—Taxonomic category beyond species. Sometimes refered to as subspecies or types.

Tick-borne—Carried by a tick.

Topography—The surface features of a place or region.

Vector—A carrier.

Virulence—The degree of disease-causing capability of a microbe.

Zoonosis—A disease that is carried and maintained in wildlife and affects people and domesticated animals.

Bibliography

Alcamo, I. Edward. *Fundamentals of Microbiology,* 6th edition. Sudbury, Mass.: Jones and Bartlett Publishers International, 2001.

Allan, Brian F., Felicia Keesing, and Richard S. Ostfeld. "Effect of Forest Fragmentation on Lyme Disease Risk." *Conservation Biology* 17, no. 1 (February 2003) 267.

Anderson, John F. "Mammalian and Avian Reservoirs for *Borrelia burgdorferi.*" *Annals of the New York Academy of Sciences* 539 (1988):180–191.

Andrea's Story. The Lyme Disease Quilt Page *http://www.angelfire.com/ny2/James/page8.html.*

Barbour, Alan G. *Lyme Disease: The Cause, The Cure, The Controversy.* Baltimore, Md.: The Johns Hopkins University Press, 1996.

Barthold, S.W. et al. "Lyme Borreliosis in the Laboratory Mouse" in *Lyme Disease: Molecular and Immunologic Approaches,* edited by Steven E. Schutzer. Cold Spring Harbor, N.Y.: Cold Spring Harbor Laboratory Press, 1992.

Batzing, Barry L. *Microbiology—An Introduction.* Pacific Grove, Calif.: Brooks/Cole, 2002.

Brundtland, Gro Harlem. "State of the World's Vaccines and Immunizations." *JAMA* 288 no. 20 (2002): 2532.

Burnet, Frank Macfarlane. *Natural History of Infectious Disease.* 3rd edition. Cambridge, England: Cambridge University Press, 1962.

Centers for Disease Control and Prevention (CDC) Lyme Disease Home Page *http://www.cdc.gov/ncidod/dvbid/lyme/index.htm.*

Centers for Disease Control and Prevention, "Southern Tick-Associated Rash Illness." *http://www.cdc.gov/ncidod/dvbid/stari/index.htm.*

Centers for Disease Control and Prevention. Vector-Borne Infectious Disease Division. *http://www.edc.gov/ncidod/dvbid/lyme/riskmap.htm.*

Cochran, G. and Paul W. Ewald. 1999. "High-Risk Defenses." *Natural History.* 108 no. 1 (1999).

Cooke, Robert. "A Plague On All Our Houses." *Popular Science* (January 1996): 51–56.

Crichton, Michael. *Prey.* New York: Harper Collins Publishers, 2002.

Cunha, Burke A. "Overdiagnosing and Overtreating Lyme Disease." *Emergency Medicine.* (August 1994): 30–36.

"Fighting Lyme Disease With Tick Bait Boxes." *Newtown (Connecticut) Bee.* June 14, 2002.

Hooper, Judith. 1999. "The New Germ Theory." *The Atlantic Monthly* 283 no. 2 (February 1999): 41–44.

Jones, Charles R. *Lyme Disease Symposium.* New Milford High School, New Milford, Conn. May 10, 2003.

Kilpatrick, Howard. Connecticut Department of Environmental Protection. Phone conversation. January 23, 2003.

Lang, Joel. "Catching the bug: How scientists found the cause of Lyme disease and why we're not out of the woods yet." *Connecticut Medicine* 53 no. 6 (1989): 357–364.

Line, Les. "'3 BR, Forest Vu' May Have Added Feature: Lyme Disease Risk." *New York Times.* April 8, 2003, Late Edition—Final, Sec. F, p. 3, col. 2.

———. "Ticks and Moths, Not Just Oaks, Linked to Acorns." *New York Times.* April 16, 1996, Late Edition—Final, Sec. C, p. 1 , col. 5.

Lyme Disease Foundation
www.lyme.org.

Magnarelli, Louis. "Laboratory Analysis for Lyme Disease." *Connecticut Medicine* 53 no. 6 (1989): 331–334.

Middleton, Donald B. "Not All Tick-Borne Illness Is Lyme Disease." *Emergency Medicine.* (August 13–22, 1994).

Nearing, Helen and Scott. *Living The Good Life.* New York: Schocken Books, 1970.

Neergaard, Lauran. "Lyme Vaccine Victims? FDA Holds Hearing on Side Effects." Feb. 1, 2001. Accessed at: *http://more.abcnews.go.com/sections/living/dailynews/lymevac020101.html.*

Editorial, *New York Times.* "Bambi's Mother in the Cross Hairs." December 2, 2002, Late Edition—Final, Sec. A, p. 20, col. 1.

Nocton, James J. et al. "Detection of *Borrelia Burgdorferi* DNA by Polymerase Chain Reaction in Synovial Fluid from Patients with Lyme Arthritis." *The New England Journal of Medicine* 330 no. 4 (1994): 229–234.

Bibliography

Nursing Drug Handbook News Capsule, Information on the Lyme Disease Vaccine Recall, November 21, 2002. Accessed at *www.ndhnow.com* on March 1, 2003.

Persing, David H. et al. "Detection of *Borrelia burgdorferi* DNA in Museum Specimens of *Ixodes dammini* Ticks." *Science* 249 (1990): 1420-23.

Schiavone, Louise. "FDA Panel Backs Lyme Disease Vaccine." (May 26, 1998) Accessed at *www.cnn.com* on March 1, 2003.

Schoen, Robert T. "Identification of Lyme Disease." *Rheumatic Disease Clinics of North America* 20 no. 3 (1994): 361–369.

Snow, John. *Snow on Cholera.* London: Oxford University Press, 1936.

Spielman, Andrew. "Prospects for Suppressing Transmission of Lyme Disease." *Annals of the New York Academy of Sciences* 539 (1998): 212–20.

Stafford, Kirby C. "Lyme Disease Prevention: Personal Prevention and Prospects for Tick Control." *Connecticut Medicine* 53 no. 6 (1989): 347–351.

————. Phone conversation. February 19, 2003.

Steere, Allen C. "Lyme Disease." *The New England Journal of Medicine* 321 no. 9 (1989): 586–596.

————. "Lyme Disease." *The New England Journal of Medicine* 345 no. 2 (2001): 115–125.

Stewart, Kay B. "A Quick Look At Lyme Disease." *Nursing* 24 no. 8 (1994): 41.

Telford, Sam R. 1989. *Ward's Natural Science Bulletin: Lyme Disease.* 1989.

Yannielli, Leonard C. "Teaching Lyme Disease." *Connecticut Journal of Science Education* 31 no. 1 (1992): 2.

Further Reading

Brock, Thomas D. *Microorganisms: From Smallpox to Lyme Disease.* New York: W.H. Freeman and Company, 1990.

Centers for Disease Control and Prevention. *Lyme Disease: A Public Information Guide.* Fort Collins, Colo.: CDC Division of Vector-Borne Infectious Diseases, 2000.

Lyme Disease and Associated Tick-borne Diseases, The Basics: A Plain−language Introduction To Tickborne Diseases. Unionville, Pa.: Lyme Disease Association of Southeastern Pennsylvania, 2002. Accessed at: *www.lymepa.org.*

Lyme Disease Association, Inc. *The ABCs of Lyme Disease.* Jackson, N.J.: Lyme Disease Association, Inc., 2002. Accessed at: *www.lymediseaseassociation.org.*

Milne, Lorus and Margery. *The Audubon Society Field Guide to North American Insects and Spiders.* New York: Alfred A. Knopf, 1984.

Vanderhoof-Forschner, Karen. *Everything You Need To Know About Lyme Disease.* New York: John Wiley and Sons, 1997.

Websites

Centers for Disease Control and Prevention,
Division of Vector-Borne Infectious Diseases
http://www.cdc.gov/ncidod/dvbid/dvbid.htm

Columbia University's Lyme Disease Research Studies
www.columbia-lyme.org

Connecticut Agricultural Experiment Station
www.caes.state.ct.us

Lyme Disease Association, Inc.
http:www.LymeDiseaseAssociation.org

Lyme Disease Foundation
www.lyme.org

Lyme Support Group for Teens
http://groups.yahoo.com/group/Lyme_Warriors

Lyme Support Group for Parents
http://www.egroup.com/group/Parents_of_Lyme_Kids

World Health Organization
www.who.int

Index

Index

Index

Picture Credits

About the Author

Len Yannielli is a professor of biology at Naugatuck Valley Community College in Waterbury, Connecticut, where he teaches microbiology, human biology, and environmental science. He is presently engaged in ecological research on Navarino Island in the Cape Horn Archipelago of Chile.

About the Editor

The late **I. Edward Alcamo** was a Distinguished Teaching Professor of Microbiology at the State University of New York at Farmingdale. Alcamo studied biology at Iona College in New York and earned his M.S. and Ph.D. degrees in microbiology at St. John's University, also in New York. He taught at Farmingdale for more than 30 years. In 2000, Alcamo won the Carski Award for Distinguished Teaching in Microbiology, the highest honor for microbiology teachers in the United States. He was a member of the American Society for Microbiology, the National Association of Biology Teachers, and the American Medical Writers Association. Alcamo authored numerous books on the subjects of microbiology, AIDS, and DNA technology as well as the award-winning textbook *Fundamentals of Microbiology*, now in its sixth edition.